We Have Also A More Sure Word Of Prophecy
2 Peter 1:19

—m—

William Bergsma

To our friend Lyde

William Bergsma

We Have Also A More Sure Word Of Prophecy 2 Peter 1:19
by William Bergsma

Printed in the United States of America

ISBN 978-1-60266-063-2

www.xulonpress.com

Foreword

—∿—

W hen CNN aired the Global Summit as part of the Bill Clinton "Global Initiative", called "in God's Name" moderated by the well-known Christiane Amanpour, all speakers of this "Forum" discussed and tried to understand why there is so much violence, disease, hunger and terrorism in the world today as never before. While all the speakers searched for answers and possible solutions to make a better world, no one realized that God has all the answers written in His Holy Bible. Jesus says in Matthew 24:37, *"But as the days of Noah were, so shall also the coming of the Son of Man be."* Jesus says this as well in Luke 17:26.

Genesis 6:12 tells us what it was like in Noah's days, *"and God looked upon the earth, and, behold, it was corrupt;"* and in verse 13, *"for the earth is filled with violence."* This is how it will be again, just before "the Son of man", Jesus, returns. Today we can already see the beginning of this violence.

Jesus also mentioned in Revelation 12:12, how bad it will get just before Jesus returns saying, *"Woe to the inhabitants of the earth for the devil is come down unto you, having great wrath, because he knoweth that he hath but a short time."*

Jesus also expects us to know when His return is near, as written in Matthew 24:33, *"So likewise ye, when ye shall see all these things, know that it is near, even at the doors."* Jesus mentioned the same thing also in Mark 13:29 and in Luke 21:31. He also says we will know that His coming is near in Luke 21:31, "Jerusalem shall be trodden down by the Gentiles, until the time of the Gentiles be fulfilled." Jerusalem was not in Israeli hands for nearly 2500 years; from the time that Nebuchadnezzar took Jerusalem in 586 BC, until 1967.

Besides the previously mentioned violence, disease, hunger, and terrorism in today's world, there is also the threat of global warming, which will cause extensive flooding in low lying areas. Bill Clinton emphasized this last year when he was on a speaking tour all across the world. He said that unless we do something drastic about pollution, lower Manhattan will be under water within 25 years. He also asked if the world would take notice? No!

There are of course many more low lying areas in the world, like the Netherlands, my country of birth, where 1/3 of the country lies below sea level. Some Dutch engineers said last year, during a news interview on TV, that the dikes built after the 1953 flood, could break again anytime if the ocean levels continue to rise due to global warming.

Closer to home, the mayor of Delta, British Columbia said recently in a news conference that she will immediately start strengthening the levees around Delta partly because the ground is slowly sinking, and partly out of concern for any future rise in the ocean's water level.

Al Gore this year also warned of dire consequences from Global warming as he made the movie "The Unthinkable Truth." This is a movie showing catastrophic consequences from climate changes if we do not stop polluting the atmosphere now.

Finally, just recently, the Prime Minister of England, Tony Blair, warned of a world catastrophe in our lifetime due to global warming causing increased flooding and hurricanes.

Jesus warned us about this, when He said in Luke 21:25, *"Upon the earth distress of nations with perplexity: the sea and waves roaring."* Jesus is referring here to our time today, when He says in Luke 21:36, *"Watch you therefore always, that you may be accounted worthy to escape* (the rapture) *all these things, that shall come to pass, and to stand before the son of man."*

"All these things" are the previously mentioned events that are happening already, or will happen soon, in the world today.

However, mankind refuses to ask God for guidance to solve the problems in to-day's world, but wants to do it themselves. Since we are unable to do this, mankind will choose a world dictator, the anti-christ, who will sign a peace treaty for 7 years with "many nations" as described in Daniel 9:27. Nations that are at war presently, or will be threatened by war in the near future. Amillennialist do not take this literally. They do not believe in the rapture, or that afterwards, when millions of people have suddenly vanished from the earth, the world economy will collapse, so that even gold and silver will be worthless, as indicated in Revelation 18:11-17.

Then the anti-christ and his false prophet will force all inhabitants of the earth to have a mark on their forehead or in their right hand. No one will be able to buy or sell, unless they have this "mark of the beast – 666," Revelation 13:16-18. After the rapture this world dictator, the anti-christ, will come to power from the European Union, being a revised "Roman Empire," as foretold in Daniel 2:40-43. He will rule the whole world with an iron fist, yet all nations will follow him, since he is able to make peace with the nations that will be at war. After 3 ½ years, Russia will break this peace treaty, and attack Israel with Iran (Persia) and Libya, using atomic warfare. But the attacking army will be pushed back to Siberia. Then Russia will attack Israel for a second time, with the help of China and other Oriental nations, who will come across the Euphrates River with 200,000,000 soldiers.

At the same time other Arab nations will also attack Israel, where the anti-christ has his headquarters in Jerusalem. Then the battle of "Armageddon" will start, when all these nations come up against Jerusalem. Zechariah 14:2 tells us that Jerusalem will be temporarily taken and partly destroyed.

However, at that time, Jesus will return to the "Mount of Olives" as King of Kings, and Lord of Lords, to set up His 1000 year millennium kingdom on earth in Jerusalem. Then there will finally be peace on the earth, that is, until Satan will be released for a short while at the end of the 1000 years for one more battle, until he is forever destroyed as in Revelation, 20:10.

In the following chapters I will deal with all the events mentioned here in detail from the Bible. I believe God's word tells us the truth about all of these events. I myself did not know much about all of this for many years, since I was a member of a Christian Reformed Church for nearly 60 years, and these events from the Bible were never clearly taught or understood, and therefore never discussed, as they should have been.

This is because the Christian Reformed Church, being Amillennialist, does not believe in the rapture, or the 7 year tribulation period when the anti-christ will be revealed for the first time to the world, and comes into power.

Jesus calls this time, "the great tribulation" in Matthew 24:21-30. *"For then shall be great tribulation, such as was not since the beginning of the world to this time, no, nor ever shall be ... Immediately after the tribulation of those days ... shall appear the sign of the Son of man in heaven."* It should be clear from these verses, that Jesus says that there will be only one "Great" tribulation just before He returns.

Amillennialist also do not believe, that during these 7 years of tribulation, the four horse men of the Apocalypse will start riding on earth, as is described in the book of Revelation. One third of mankind will be destroyed from pestilence, hunger, war and terrorism, which we can clearly see already beginning today. Also, according to their book, the "CRC Viewpoint," Amillennialist do not believe that Revelation 20:4, *"they lived and reigned with Christ a thousand years,"* is to be taken literally, as I will deal with later in one of the following chapters.

Another issue I will deal with in this book is the theology that replaces Israel in the Bible with the church. This "Replacement Theology" is commonly taught by the CRC whereby the promises made by God to Israel, become promises to the church.

At this point I will just refer to a letter from William E. Sutter, the executive director of "The Friends of Israel." In a letter dated April 2002, he writes, "The movement, popularly known as Replacement Theology, is teaching about Israel's place in God's program. In simple terms, this perversion of theology insists that there is no place for Israel in the current biblical scheme of things. The church becomes Israel, and the literal and historic promises God made to the Chosen people – including those made concerning their land – are rescinded, spiritualized, and given to the Christian church. The net effects of denying Scripture's clear teaching about Israel results in a great confusion about prophetic revelation. However, it is prophetic revelation that clarifies current trends on the world stage and outlines future events."

Also, in the "Israel Report" from March/April 2000 I read, "This is where centuries of unscriptural 'Replacement Theology' have taken most of Christendom. One of the main causes for current confusion in understanding prophecy is the failure to take Israel related prophecies literally."

—〰—

This book is dedicated with much love and gratitude
to Jim and Leanne

for all their hard work in getting this book published.

With much appreciation,

Dad

We have also a more sure word of prophecy
2 Peter 1:19

written by William Bergsma

—〰—

WE HAVE ALSO A MORE SURE WORD OF PROPHECY

—⁓—

Preface

—⟋m⟍—

For nearly 60 years, my wife and I have been members of a Christian Reformed Church. We were baptized and did confession of faith in a CRC church in Holland. After coming to Canada in 1953, we got married in a CRC church in Brampton, Ontario which just had been built.

Shortly after that, when Georgetown also needed a CRC church, we helped with the establishment and the building of that church, which started as only a small group at first. Later, in 1979, after moving to the west coast, and with only a dozen people, we started a CRC church in Nanaimo, BC. When this congregation grew, we began to help with the construction of this church as well.

Although in all these churches we faithfully participated in the Bible studies from the church, we somehow never ever talked about or studied the prophecies, or talked about what the Bible had to say about the rapture, the battle of Armageddon, the four horsemen in Revelation, the anti-christ, the millennium, etc., as if these events did not even exist. They were more or less completely ignored, or considered to be irrelevant.

For this reason we knew practically nothing about all of this, until we came across a television program from the Jack Van Impe Ministries. Here we heard, for the first time, what the Bible says about all these things and what will happen when Jesus returns; the rapture, the start of the 7 year tribulation, the anti-christ, the battle of Armageddon, and the millennium. After having listened to his programs for a time, we received such a blessing from it that we decided to become partners of faith with the Jack Van Impe Ministries, and support Rexella and Jack Van Impe with their ministry as much as we possibly could. At a time and age when most preachers are thinking of retirement, Jack Van Impe celebrated his 59th year in the ministry, and not only kept going, but in January of 2006, they added another 104 late night TV stations, in addition to all the regular stations that were on the air already. These late night broadcasts were added after a survey showed that millions of people are watching TV during the late night hours between midnight and 6 a.m. providing a great opportunity to spread the gospel even more, to millions of people, about being prepared for the soon coming of Jesus Christ. They explained things like the rapture, and the fact that it will be followed by the tribulation period with all the terrible things mentioned in Revelation.

About the rapture; would it not make sense that a caring and loving God would take us home before this terrible tribulation starts? The rapture would give millions of people another chance to believe in Christ, because after witnessing the rapture, they would now see that all the Bible had said about what would happen in the future, had come true as prophesied in God's word.

One might ask why it is so important that we should know all this about the rapture, the tribulation, the anti-christ, and the millennium? We could ask in return, why would the Lord have told the prophets, and all the other authors of the books of the Bible to write this, if it was not important for us to know all this. The important thing is to know what the correct interpretation is of all these events as written in God's word.

How do we interpret the rapture, the tribulation, the four horsemen, the battle of Armageddon, the anti-christ, and the millennium, etc.? What is the correct interpretation? Whatever our interpretation is of these events, we should at least be able to discuss this together as brothers and sisters in Christ in the same church, rather than be forced out of the CRC church.

Rev. Anthony A. Hoekema is a spokesman for the CRC Viewpoint (CRC Viewpoint presents the view of the Christian Reformed Church on practical problems of the Christian faith and life.) Rev. Hoekema says in CRC Viewpoint' "We should note at this point that the Christian Reformed Church has refused to recognize either type of premillennialism as a valid option for its members." In 1917 the Reverend M. H. Bultema, then pastor of the First Christian Reformed Church of Muskegon, Michigan published a book entitled "Maranatha," in which he defended the dispensational position. The Christian Reformed Synod of 1918, after examining Bultema's views found him to be in conflict with the creeds on two points: he taught that the church did not exist until the coming of Christ, and that Christ was not king of the church, but only king of Israel. Since Bultema did not retract these views, he was deposed." Rev. Hoekema also said: "In 1946, in fact D. H. Kromminga, a professor at Calvin Seminary, recognized that his premillennial views were in conflict with article 37 of the Belgic Confession... since he believed in a future millennium after Christ's return... he appealed to Synod for a judgment regarding the scriptural validity of his article... but he died before the matter could be resolved."

I am really shocked to read that some good Christian people, because they took God's word literally, were forced out of the CRC church, the church that my wife and I have faithfully supported for over 50 years. Why could the CRC not just discuss these matters as brothers and sisters in Christ, and then let a member that believes the Bible literally stay with the CRC if they so desire? Of course, Kromminga, being a professor at Calvin Seminary, would not be allowed to instruct future ministers to take the Bible literally as God's word. However, taking into consideration what Jesus said in Matthew 24:33, *"So, likewise ye, when ye shall see all these things, know that it is near, even at the door,"* more members are starting to take God's word literally. They do not want to openly admit it however, because they are not ready to leave their church of a lifetime behind yet.

Therefore, my reason for writing this book is to see what God's word says. Should we read the Bible literally as the dispensationalist do, or interpret the Bible passages privately by comparing it to other Bible passages from the scripture as the Amillennialist do. Do we base our interpretations on the word of God, or upon previously accepted religious doctrines? Rev. Anthony A. Hoekema says in CRC Viewpoint, "We Amillennialist teach that the thousand year millennium of Revelation 20:4-6 is not an earthly reign at all, but a reign of deceased believers with Christ in heaven. Amillennialist do not understand the thousand years in a strictly literal sense… we interpreted the expression 'a thousand years' to mean a very long time. This period extends from the first coming of Christ (the beginning of Satan's defeat in John 12:30–32), to just before the second coming of Christ."

First of all, why can we not take it literally, as Revelation 20:22-6 says, *"We shall reign with Christ a thousand years?"* Why change God's words to "a very long time" when it clearly says "a thousand years"?

Rev. Verbrugge in his sermons about Revelation says, "The millennium is not a thousand years; Christ will reign from His ascension till He returns. The so-called 1000 years are symbolic. We are called to reign over this earth right here, right now. When Jesus walked on earth, He brought the kingdom of God here on earth; therefore the kingdom of God has already come. We live and reign with Christ right now, right here."

Here we have two totally different Amillennialist views of the millennium, as Hoekema says "a reign with the deceased believers in heaven," while Verbrugge says, "When Jesus walked on the earth, He brought the kingdom of God, and we are called to reign with Christ over the earth right now." Why should the Amillennialist say this, when the Bible clearly says in Revelation 20:4-6, *"and they lived and reigned with Christ a thousand years"*? And about it not being an earthly reign, as Hoekema says, Revelation 20:7-8 tells us, *"and when the thousand years are expired, Satan will be loosed out of his prison and shall go out to deceive the nations which are in the four quarters of the earth."* From this verse it should be clear that the thousand year millennium is on earth. Because verse 8 says it is "on earth," it could not mean heaven, as Rev. Hoekema says in CRC Viewpoint; "Deceased believers with Christ in heaven."

Why can we not simply believe what the Bible says? Revelation begins with *"The Revelation of Jesus Christ...3... Blessed is he that readeth, and they that hear the words of this prophecy, and keep those things which are written therein: for the time is at hand."* The third verse from the end of the book, Revelation 22:19 says, *"And if any man shall take away from the words in this book of this prophecy, God shall take away his part out of this book of life, and out of the holy city, and from the things, which are written in this book."*

These are very serious words spoken here and gives us therefore, even more reason to take these words literally, as the apostle Peter says in 2 Peter 1:19, *"We have a more sure word of prophecy; whereunto you do well that ye take heed,* (take these words seriously)*... 20. Knowing this first, that no prophecy of the scripture is of any private interpretation. 21. For the prophecy came not in old time by the will of man; but holy men of God spake as they were moved by the Holy Ghost."* How then, do we honestly interpret the apostle's words, "no scripture is of any private interpretation"? Does this mean that we can just change "a thousand years," into "a very long time" as Hoekema says? Rev. Hoekema further says, "How do we Amillennialist interpret the binding of Satan as described in Revelation 20:1-3?" He continues with "We believe that Satan was bound by Christ at the beginning of Christ's earthly ministry, Matthew 12:29' 'How can one enter a strong mans house and plunder his goods, unless he first binds the strong man'?" How can one compare this to the binding of Satan? If I had a choice to make, I would definitely choose the literal interpretation of the binding of Satan, as in Revelation 20:1-3; and believe in God's word in Revelation 20:2 where it says, *"And he laid hold of the dragon, that old serpent* (as in the garden of Eden*), which is the Devil, and Satan, and bound him a thousand years. 3 And cast him into a bottomless pit, and shut him up, and set a seal upon him, that he should deceive the nations no more, till the thousand years should be fulfilled, and after that he must be loosed a little season."* Why not simply accept what the Lord says here, that Satan will be bound for a thousand years? Does that not look much more acceptable, than the strong man from Matthew 12:29? Is it any wonder therefore, that so many have become dispensationalist and interpret the Bible literally?

However, this is not how Rev. Vander Waal sees it. After a trip to Canada, and after a discussion with Rev. Raymond J. Sikkema of the Christian Reformed Church in St. Catherines, Vander Waal wrote his book, "Lindsay and Bible Prophecies." He quoted the book of Psalms saying, "If I forget you, O Jerusalem (Psalm 137:5) peace be in Israel (Psalms 125:5)." He continues with, "We should apply this text to the church, but the dispensationalist read them as pointing to the restoration of Israel, and the golden future of a Palestinian Jerusalem." He further says, "Israel remained God's covenant people, until He (God) took that privileged status away in the year 70 AD." (I will get into detail about

70 AD later in the book). Vander Waal also says, "We must also break with the notion that there is some sort of special future in store for the Jews. ... Lindsay likes to talk about the 'rebirth of Israel'; by this he means the return of the Jews to Palestine, their homeland. This perspective on Israel represents a colossal secularizing of the meaning of the biblical prophesies." (Contrary to Reverend Vander Waal's statement, almost all of the prophets in the Bible prophesied that the Jews would come back to their homeland, as we will see later in this book.)

Vander Waal further says, "This realization requires breaking with Jewish misconceptions including the false belief that the restoration of the Jewish nation is a sign that the end is near. Jesus shows how the Lord finally dismisses Jerusalem, the city that slaughtered the Lamb. Henceforth He will no longer recognize the Jews as His people." What Vander Waal is saying here is that the Lord has abandoned His chosen people the Jews. However it was not the Lord who said this but the Amillennialist.

On the cover of the book: "The American Prophecy," written by the well-known bestselling author Michael D. Evans, I read, "If you abandon Israel, God will never forgive you." This is a very powerful statement, which we should take very seriously, especially in the light of what we just read from Reverend Vander Waal. Unfortunately, he is not the only Amillennialist with this opinion, because Rev. Hoekema says in CRC Viewpoint, "The teaching that God has a separate purpose for Israel, and for the church, is in error, though this concept dominates dispensational theology and is not in harmony with the New Testament teaching... if the New Testament church is now God's holy nation, what room is left for the emerge during the millennium of another holy nation, distinct from the church?" Rev. Hoekema continues with "Dispensationalists often appeal to Romans 11 to support their view on Israel" and further says "Remember however, that even if we were inclined to understand verses 25-27 as teaching a future conversion of Israel, we would still have to admit that Romans 11 says nothing whatsoever about a regathering of Israel to its land, or about a future role of Christ over a millennium Israelite kingdom."

How can there not be a future conversion, and a re-gathering of Israel, as well as a future role of Christ over a millennial kingdom, when God says in Ezekiel 38:16, *"And thou shalt come up against my people of Israel, as a cloud to cover the land, it shall be in the latter days, and I will bring thee against my land, that the heathen may know me, when I shall be sanctified in thee, O Gog, before their eyes."?* The Lord says here that the armies of Gog (Russia) will come up against "My land," as He calls Israel, in the "Latter days", just before Jesus returns. Why would the Lord call Israel "My land" here in Ezekiel, if He has dismissed His chosen people Israel? Who would these armies be attacking if God had not re-gathered His people to their homeland? Who is God defending here?

Consider what is now happening in the Middle East at this very moment, in Iran, Iraq, Syria, Lebanon, etc. Even the secular media, who do not believe that God is in control of the world situation today, see the threatening clouds of war. In the September 11, 2006 issue of Time magazine, there is a cover story article entitled, "Its Not Over Yet" by military historian Max Boot that sums up the sobering situation today, five years after September 11, 2001. The article states, "Iraq is slipping deeper into the blood-red waters of civil strife. The Taliban is resurgent in Afghanistan. Hizballah is crowing in the wake of Israel's inconclusive attacks. Hamas runs the Palestinian Authority. Iran is drawing closer to acquiring nuclear weapons. Osama Bin Laden and his deputy Ayman al-Zawahiri, continue to taunt the West with messages of defiance, and jihadist cells from London to Lahore plot fresh attacks." "Its not over yet." Time magazine Sept. 11, 2006

As in Luke 21:31, *"So like wise ye, when you see all these things come to pass, know ye that the kingdom of God is nigh at hand."* (Similarly in Matthew 24:32-33) This saying of Jesus does not contradict Matthew 24:36, *"But of that day and hour knoweth no man."* We simply don't know the exact day and hour, but we can certainly tell from the signs that the time is near. One of those signs is definitely the fact that the Jews started coming back to their homeland in 1948.

Now that they are back, we can expect the rapture at any time, followed by the 7 year tribulation when the anti-christ is revealed. Then all the countries listed in Ezekiel will come up against Jerusalem for the battle of "Armageddon," where the Lord Himself will defeat them when He returns to Jerusalem to set up His millennial kingdom. I will get into detail about all these events in the following chapters and especially about the re-gathering of the Jews to their homeland.

As for Romans not mentioning this, read Romans 11:25-27 again, verse 26 reads, *"And so all Israel shall be saved, as it is written, there shall come out of Zion the deliverer, and shall turn away ungodliness from Jacob."* It was the Lord Himself who changed Jacob's name to Israel in Genesis 35:10, *"And God said unto him, Thy name is Jacob: thy name shall not be called any more Jacob, but Israel shall be thy name, and he called his name Israel."*

Continuing with Romans 11:27, *"For this is my covenant unto them, when I shall take away their sins."* Furthermore, the Lord promises an everlasting covenant with Israel in almost all of the books of the Bible as in Genesis 17:7, *"And I will establish my covenant between Me and thee, and to thy seed after thee, in their generations for an everlasting covenant, to be a God unto thee, and to thy seed after thee. 8. And I will give unto thee, and to thy seed after thee, the land wherein thou art a stranger, all the land of Canaan for an everlasting possession: and I will be their God."* The Lord

could not have said it more plainly in this passage of the
Bible, that the Lord has indeed an everlasting special purpose
for the Jews; that the Jews will inherit Canaan forever.

Rev. Hoekema says, "Then how can Paul be teaching us,
that God still has a special purpose for the Jews and a separate future for Israel"? As we have just seen in Gen. 17:7, the
Jews and their seed after them have indeed a special future
in Israel. The prophet Amos says in Amos 9:14 *"And I will
bring again the captivity of my people Israel...15. And I will
plant them upon their land, and they shall no more be pulled
up out of their land which I have given them, saith the Lord
thy God."* No more pulled out of their land, means the Jews
will have the land of Israel forever. Not only Joel and Amos,
but also all the Old Testament prophets tell us that the Jews
will come back to their homeland after having been scattered
through all the nations. This happened officially in May
1948, almost 2500 years after king Nebuchadnezzar took the
people of Israel captive. The Jews got back their own land of
Israel, officially through the United Nations, as the Lord had
prophesied through His prophets all through the Bible.

Peter says in 2 Peter 1:19, *"We have a more sure word of
prophecy."* Also, we read in Jeremiah 30:3, *"For, lo, the days
come, saith the Lord, that I will bring again the captivity of
my people Israel and Judah, saith the Lord: and I will cause
them to return to the land that I gave to their fathers, and
they shall possess it."*

Rev. Verbrugge, in his sermons from Revelation says,
"Scripture does not talk about the rapture and the rapture does
not hold up to the scrutiny of the scriptures." Contrary to this,
Rev. Hoekema says in CRC Viewpoint, "The Amillennialist
do believe in the rapture, but we believe that after this joyous
meeting in the air, the raised and transformed believers will
go back with Christ to the earth." He continues with, "the
believers will enter into everlasting glory on the new earth,"
and says "the Bible clearly teaches we will live in resur-

rected bodies on a new earth (Isaiah 65:17, 2 Peter 3:3, Rev. 2:11)." Further to that, in Isaiah 65:20 we read, *"There shall be no more thence an infant of days, nor an old man that hath not filled his days: for the child shall die an hundred years old: but the sinner being an hundred years old shall be accursed."* According to this verse, there will still be sin on the new earth. Rev. Hoekema stated in CRC Viewpoint, "We will enter into everlasting glory on a new earth, where the wolf will live with lamb, however the Old Testament does not point to a thousand year period before the end." If this is so, as Hoekema says, how then do I interpret Isaiah 65:20, where we live in this glorious new earth, where the wolf will live with the lamb, yet there will be sin? That there will be sin on this new earth is also shown in Revelation 16, where, at the end of the thousand year reign with Christ, Satan, for a short while, will revolt with these sinners on the new earth against Christ, before Satan will be destroyed according to Rev. 20:10.

If we do not believe in a thousand year reign with Christ in the millennium as Rev. Hoekema, Rev. Verbrugge, and Rev. Vander Waal are saying, in what period of time is it then, that the wolf will live with the lamb on a glorious new earth, where there is however still sin? This time could not point to heaven, because there will never be sin in heaven as the scriptures clearly say. Also, it could not be on this present earth, because the wolf cannot live with the lamb in peace yet, since Christ has not yet returned and therefore the animals have not changed. However, since the prophet Isaiah clearly says, the wolf will live with the lamb in peace, and at the same time there will be sinners on this new earth, it should therefore be absolutely clear, that the only place where this could happen, would be during the 1000 year millennium, when we will reign with Christ on this new earth, as the Bible says in Rev. 20:4, and also as the prophet Isaiah says in Isaiah 65:20.

Rev. Verbrugge says, "Jesus teaches that the church will go through the tribulation." How then do I read in Rev. 3:10, *"I also will keep you from the hour of temptation, which shall come upon all the world, to them that dwell upon the earth"?* It should be clear from this passage, that the Lord will rapture us before the tribulation begins (the hour of temptation as the Lord says). Jesus says, "I will keep you from the hour of temptation, which shall come..." meaning it is in the future, and therefore this hour of temptation could not be something that is happening all the time, as the Amillennialist say. Jesus says, "upon all the world" referring to the great tribulation of Matthew 24:21.

Why can we not take this all literally as God's word? Would it be so difficult to believe, that a loving God would not let His children go through the terrible time of tribulation, but instead will rapture us? But then, do the Amillennialist believe in the "great tribulation" of Matthew 24:21? Why is the great tribulation not interpreted by the Amillennialist for the time of the end, as Jesus clearly says in Matthew 24:21? I will deal with this later, but Rev. Hoekema says in CRC Viewpoint, "Amillennialist believe that the return of Christ will be preceded by certain signs: the preaching of the gospel to all nations, the great tribulation, the great apostasy or rebellion, and the coming of a personal anti-christ; but we do not believe that these events will take place only in the time just before Christ's return, for they have been present in some sense from the very beginning of the Christian era, and are present now". The Bible clearly says that the tribulation is for the time of the end. We will look at the passages of scripture that deal with this later.

Rev. Verbrugge says, "The dispensationalist view of the rapture, and the seven year tribulation, and the plagues stir up the imagination ... does not hold up to the creationist view of the church." As for the church, many churches believe that these views do hold up to the creationist view. Vander Waal adds to this, "Three and a half years after the rapture comes the great tribulation, the time of great oppression. This is an axiom from Hal Lindsey. The talk of Babylon and the beast fits into this period. This axiom too must be rejected. It is thoroughly unscriptural." On page 42-43 of his book, he says, "we must resist the temptation to lift an intriguing text out of its context, and make it part of our apocalyptic collage." This applies to Matthew 24:15-21 just as much as Jeremiah 30:7 which says, *"Alas! for that day is great, so that none is like it: it is even the time of Jacob's trouble; but he shall be saved out of it."* (Since the Lord Himself told Jacob that his name will be Israel from now on, Jacob's trouble therefore means Israel's trouble, as in Genesis 35:10.

Rev. Vander Waal continues with, "The passage in Matthew 24:15-21 deals with the anxious days before the destruction of Jerusalem in 70 AD. This is clear from the term Jesus uses 'those who are in Judea,' (Vs. 16), 'pray that your flight may not be in winter or on a Sabbath' (vs. 20). The text itself rules out the prospect of applying this passage to the distant future, and the text must be our guide after all. The first place in the New Testament where we read about the great tribulation is Matthew 24:21…only when we insist on reading Matthew 24 in the light of a telescope are we forced to conclude that Jesus was talking about something other than the destruction of Jerusalem. Lindsey places the 'desolating sacrilege' not in the Herodian temple of Jesus time, but in the rebuilt temple after the rapture. The great tribulation is also likewise scheduled for this time after the rapture." He goes on to say, "And so the tribulation axiom lives on…the way is open for the tribulation bogeyman that haunts so many Christians in their outlook on the future…as the tribulation is worked out, the rule of thumb seems to be the zanier the better. The result is fiction, speculation."

He wrote this on page 77 of his book and I had to look twice to make sure that I did read this right. Who is the bogeyman here? Jesus talks about the tribulation in Matthew 24:21. And just a few verses earlier in Matthew 24:15, Jesus talks about the "abomination that maketh desolate" which refers to the end time as described in 2 Thessalonians 2:4, when the anti-christ blasphemes the name of God in the new temple in Jerusalem, which has to be built yet, just before Jesus returns.

Rev. Vander Waal further says; "In Christ's prophecy recorded in Matthew 24, the 'desolating sacrilege' mentioned by Daniel in his prophecy about the time of Antiochus Epiphanes (Daniel 9:27) becomes a reference to the manifest apostasy of the Jewish covenant people." Vander Waal here interprets "the abomination that maketh desolate," which Jesus mentioned in Matthew 24:15, as a "sacrilege" in the Old Testament temple, which was desecrated by Antiochus Epiphanes but misses the fact that Jesus is pointing to the future desecration of the temple by the anti-christ, which will be much worse.

Matthew 24:14, *"And this gospel of the kingdom shall be preached in all the world for a witness unto all nations; and then shall the end come. 15. When ye therefore shall see the abomination of desolation, spoken of by the prophet Daniel, stand in the holy place... 16... flee into the mountains... 21. for then shall be great tribulation such as was not since the beginning of the world..."*

When Jesus speaks of "the abomination of desolation," in Matthew 24:15, He refers specifically to that "spoken of by the prophet Daniel." He speaks without question in the future tense, that this has not happened yet, but shall happen at the end. He states the fact that this abomination will "stand in the holy place." He is not speaking in the past tense about something historical. He is not referring to Antiochus Epiphanes at all, but a future occurrence of "the abomination of desolation" defiling the temple. Then Jesus says, in Matthew 24:21, *"For then shall be great tribulation, such as was not since the beginning of the world, no, nor ever shall be,"* and continuing in verse 29, *"immediately after the tribulation of those days shall the sun be darkened and the moon shall not give her light, and the stars shall fall from heaven, and then shall appear the sign of the Son of Man in Heaven."*

How much more clearly does Jesus need to spell it out? How could Jesus' words possibly be interpreted as being Antiochus Epiphanes in 200 BC or the destruction of Jerusalem and the Herodian temple in 70 AD? The abomination of Antiochus Epiphanes happened more than 200 years before Christ spoke of "the abomination" in reference to signs of his return and the end of the world. (Matthew 24:3) Vander Waal says the sacrilege happened in the Herodian temple roughly 70 AD, some 2000 years ago, but instead, contrary to this, Jesus says in Matthew 24:29 that immediately after the tribulation of those days, the sun will be darkened, the stars will fall from heaven, and the sign of the Son of Man (Jesus) appears. Since the sun has not darkened yet, and the stars have not fallen from heaven, and most importantly, Jesus has not yet appeared, how then could Matthew 24:15-29 be interpreted as pointing to the Herodian temple? Instead, this abomination is the same "man of sin ... that son on perdition" Paul speaks about in 2 Thessalonians 2:4.

Therefore everything Jesus mentioned in Matthew 24 was written for the future as indications of Jesus' return and the end of the world. Many of all these events are happening in the world today, they could be fulfilled soon, when Jesus returns with the rapture. How did Vander Waal's book, with this interpretation of Matthew 24:15-29 get past the scrutiny of Calvin Seminary? Or, do all Amillennialist agree with this interpretation of Matthew 24:15-29? If this is so, it is no wonder that Bultema and Krommiga did not agree with the Amillennialist views of God's word.

Again, this is the reason for me writing this book, so that we together as Amillennialist and dispensationalist, can study, and see what the Lord says in His word about all the events like the rapture, the tribulation, the four horsemen, the anti-christ, the millennium, etc. In the next chapters, we will search the scriptures, to find out what God's word tells us.

During a visit to New Orleans, with regard to hurricane Katrina, Billy Graham was asked about the world's problems. He replied, "National and International peace will come, I believe, when Jesus comes as the Messiah." When he was asked when that will be, Billy Graham said "We are not to set dates, but Jesus gave us the signs to look for, and nearly all of them are being fulfilled right now." As Jesus said in Matthew 24:33, *"So likewise ye, when you shall see all these things, know that it is near, even at the door."*

The signs, "these things," as Jesus said, are very obvious in the world today, like the worst hurricanes and tornados we've ever had, as in Luke 21:25 *"the sea and the waves roaring."* There are new kinds of diseases today as in Matthew and in Luke 21:11 *"And great earthquakes shall be in diverse places, and famines, and pestilences,"* like the dreaded bird flu, that is so much in the news today. All the violence on TV and in the movies as indicated in Matthew 24:37 *"but as the days of Noah were, so shall also the coming of the Son of Man be."* How were the days of Noah? Genesis 6:11 says, *"The earth was corrupt before God, and the earth was filled with violence."* The violence is obvious everywhere today, as we see the frequent mass murders by school classmates in schools and universities in Canada and the United States. These signs indicate that, *"His return is near,"* as it says in Matthew 24:33.

Daniel 2:44 tells us, *"and in the days of these kings shall the God of heaven set up a kingdom which shall never be destroyed."*

Isaiah 35:10, *"and come to Zion with songs and everlasting joy: they shall obtain joy and gladness, and sorrow and sighing shall flee away."*

Chapter 1

"...the day of Christ is at hand."
2 Thessalonians 2:1-8

—ᘏᘏᘏ—

This passage, 2 Thessalonians 2:1-8, is an amazing and powerful part of the scriptures, where the apostle Paul talks about the rapture, the coming of Jesus Christ, and when for the first time the anti-christ will be revealed, after the rapture. The anti-christ is sitting in the future temple which has yet to be rebuilt before Jesus returns to the new earth. In verse 8, we read that the anti-christ will be destroyed with the brightness of the coming of Jesus Christ.

2 Thessalonians 2:1, *"Now we beseech you brethren, by the coming of our Lord Jesus Christ, and by our gathering together unto Him, 2. That ye be not soon shaken in mind, or be troubled, neither by spirit, nor by word, nor by letter from us, as that the day of Christ is at hand, 3. Let no man deceive you by any means: for that day shall not come, except there come a falling away first, and that man of sin be revealed, the son of perdition."*

It should be clear from this passage, that there will be a falling away before the son of perdition will be revealed. Here in 2 Thess. 2:1-2 the Thessalonians seem to have the misunderstanding that they missed the resurrection; that the day of the Lord had already begun. The apostle Paul

33

clarifies it for them. He tells them that day (the day of the Lord returning to earth) will not come, until there shall be a falling away (the rapture) and then at the same time, the man of sin (the anti-christ) will be revealed. One might ask how we know that Paul interprets "falling away" to mean the rapture? Could it not just mean falling away from the faith rather than the rapture? It does not say "falling away from the faith," rather, the Greek word "Apostasia" has been used here for "falling away", meaning "departure away from something or someone." Also, Paul refers to the rapture again in verse 7, and therefore we can be sure that the rapture is the right interpretation.

One might also ask how we know that Paul is talking here about the anti-christ, the man of sin? We know, that it could not mean Satan, because Satan was revealed already in paradise to us, and this man of sin, the man of perdition will not be revealed to us until the rapture, which has not happened yet. The anti-christ is the only man who fits this description.

Rev. Verbrugge says, "We do not believe in a personal anti-christ, every person or nation that is bad is an anti-christ." Rev. Vander Waal says, "think of their (dispensationalists) expectations of a 'special end time' as a period dominated by a cultural human monster, the anti-christ. Think also of their exegesis of Revelation, which was based on faulty assumptions." He says on page 94, "After the reformation, the belief that the anti-christ will be someone in the distant future was given up almost completely…The reformers, including Luther and Calvin, did not want to think in terms of a future anti-christ."

I can hardly believe that Luther and Calvin did not believe in a personal future anti-christ. Is this why the Amillennialist also do not think of a personal anti-christ? Contrary to this, Rev. Hoekema in CRC Viewpoint, expresses a different opinion when he says, "Amillennialist believe that the return of Christ will be preceded by certain signs: the preaching of the gospel to all the nations, the great apostasy or rebellion, and the coming of a personal anti-christ, but we do not believe that these events will take place only in the time just before Christ's return. For they have been present in some sense from the beginning of the Christian era, and are present now."

Why is it that Amillennialist simply will not believe that all these things, like the rapture, the great tribulation, the coming of the anti-christ, and the four horsemen, etc., will happen at the time of the end, but instead believe they are present all the time? The apostle Paul clearly says in 2 Thess. 2:2 that the man of sin (the anti-christ) will not be revealed until after the day of Christ's coming which has not happened yet and therefore the anti-christ could not be known yet. It is even clearer in verse 4, *"Who opposeth and exalteth himself above all that is called God, or that is worshipped; so that he* (the anti-christ) *as God sitteth in the temple of God, showing himself to be God."* Rev. Verbrugge says, "Scripture does not mention anything about the temple of the Lord to be built yet. It is insulting to think, that a palace could be built with human hands here on earth for Him to dwell in. The son of Man does not need a shack or a palace in Jerusalem to dwell in."

True, He doesn't need it, but that's not the point, and scripture does indeed tell us of the new temple. How else would I read Malachi 3:1, *"Behold, I will send my messenger, and he shall prepare the way before me: and the Lord, whom ye seek, shall suddenly come to His temple."*? The prophet clearly says here, that the Lord will suddenly come to His temple, and it is also clear form the next verse, that the temple mentioned here, is the temple to be built yet, just before Jesus returns to the new earth. Malaci 3:2 *"But who may abide the day of his coming? And who shall stand when he appeareth? For he is like a refiner's fire, and like a fuller's soap."* This obviously doesn't refer to when Jesus was born in a manger! This is the same temple the apostle Paul points to in 2 Thessalonians 2:4. It should be clear from Malachi therefore that the temple mentioned here, will be in existence when Jesus appears, and therefore has to be built yet since there is no temple yet in Jerusalem.

Also, Malachi 3:4 deals with the Jews on the new earth, after Jesus "appeareth" as he says, *"then shall the offering of Judah and Jerusalem be pleasant unto the Lord, as in the days of old, and as in former years."* It is clear that this points to the new earth, when the Jews have returned, and as the Lord Himself says, it will be again as it was in "former years." This is also clear from Isaiah 65:25, *"They shall not hurt nor destroy in all my Holy mountain, saith the Lord."* And further in Isaiah 66:1, *"Thus saith the Lord, The heaven is my throne, and the earth is my footstool: where is the house that ye built unto me? And where is the place of my rest? ... 6. A voice of noise from the city, a voice from the temple, a voice of the Lord that rendereth recompense to his enemies."* Again, it should be very clear, that after the Lord asks, "where is my house?", that the new temple has to be built yet. It could not possibly be the temple mentioned by Vander Waal, which was the temple in Herodian times which was destroyed in 70 AD, as all the next passages from the scriptures will show. This temple is in the future.

Zechariah 6:12-13, *"... Behold, the man whose name is The BRANCH (Jesus); and he shall grow up out of his place, and he shall build the temple of the Lord: 13. Even He shall build the temple of the Lord; and He shall bear the glory, and he shall sit and rule upon his throne."* It is very clear that verse 13, "He shall sit and rule upon His throne," points to the future, because it says "shall sit," referring to something that has not happened yet. This could therefore not mean His present throne in Heaven, because the Lord sits there already. Instead it points to the return of Jesus Christ, when

He will sit upon His throne in Jerusalem on the new earth, where we will reign with Christ a thousand years.

Also, Micah 4:1, *"But in the last days it shall come to pass, that the mountain of the house of the Lord shall be established...2. And many nations shall come, and say, Come , and let us go up to the mountain of the Lord, and to the house of the God of Jacob ... for the law shall go forth of Zion, and the word of the Lord from Jerusalem."* Here Micah says "the mountain of the house of the Lord," which is the mountain in Jerusalem, where the Lord will reign from, when He returns to the new earth. Also Micah says "In the last days" shall the house (temple) be established, clearly, in the future, and therefore could not be the temple from Antiochus Epiphanes, or the Herodian temple from 70 AD. We also know that it points to Jesus return because verse 3 says, "Neither shall they learn war anymore," and since Jesus has said all along that there will be wars until the end of time, until He returns, this very clearly points to the building of His temple when He returns. Verse 2 makes it even clearer, when it says "We shall walk in His paths" which will not happen until Jesus will reign on the new earth, as mentioned in verse 7, "and the Lord shall reign over them in mount Zion henceforth, even for ever."

How much clearer can the Lord tell us through His word that there will be built a new temple in Jerusalem at the time of Jesus return and that this temple will be there forever? Still, if we are in doubt, read Haggai 2:7, *"and I will shake all the nations, and the desire of all nations shall come: and I will fill this house* (temple) *with glory, saith the Lord of hosts...9. The glory of the latter house* (temple) *shall be greater than the former* (the Herodian temple) *saith the Lord of Hosts, and in this place* (the new temple in Jerusalem to be built yet) *will I give peace, saith the Lord of Hosts."* Here the Lord Himself says that the latter house (the new temple to be built when Jesus returns) will be more glorious than

37

the former (the Herodian temple before it was destroyed in 70AD). It should be very clear form the different places in the scriptures that the Lord will reign from a new temple yet to be built in Jerusalem, when He returns to the new earth. It is mentioned so many times in the Bible. Zechariah 8:3 says, *"Thus saith the Lord; I am returned unto Zion, and dwell in the midst of Jerusalem: and Jerusalem shall be called a city of truth; and the mountain of the Lord of hosts, the holy mountain."*

So much for Verbrugge saying, "The Lord does not need a shack or a palace to dwell in, the scriptures do not say anything about a temple." As we have just seen from the scriptures, they do mention everywhere that the Lord will have a temple built for Him when Jesus in about to return, when at the same time the anti-christ will be revealed as in 2 Thessalonians 2:3.

It seems to be all so simple to understand, especially in 2 Thess. 2:5, where we read, *"Remember ye not, that, when I was yet with you, I told you these things?"*

Chapter 2

2 Thessalonians 2:5

—$\sim$—

As we have seen in the previous chapter, it seems all so easy to understand, if one takes the Bible literally, like 2 Thess 2:5, where we read *"Remember ye not, that when I was yet with you, I told you these things?"*

Paul points here to Matthew 24:15 where Jesus said: *"When ye therefore shall see the abomination of desolation, spoken of by Daniel the prophet, stand in the holy place* (the new temple in Jerusalem, which will have to be built yet, before Jesus returns) *whoso readeth, let him understand."* Jesus says here "let him understand" which means that we should take Jesus' words spoken here literally. Jesus speaks highly of Daniel the prophet. Here in Matthew 24:15, Jesus is referring to what Daniel said in Daniel 9:27, *"he* (the anti-christ*) shall cause the sacrifice and the oblation to cease, and for the overspreading of abominations, he* (the anti-christ*) shall make it desolate,"* Here in Daniel 9:27, Daniel says exactly the same thing as what Jesus said in Matthew 24:15. Both Jesus and Daniel point to the same thing, namely what the apostle Paul said in 2 Thessalonians 2:4, the man of sin (the anti-christ) blaspheming the name of God in the new temple in Jerusalem. In all these places they point to the end times, when Jesus returns with the rapture, and when the anti-christ, (the son of perdition as Paul says) will blaspheme the name of God. Verbrugge says, "we are not to identify the anti-christ. The anti-christ is not a person, the anti-christ is symbolic. It is not a specific person that will show himself in the last days. Every bad person or bad nation is an anti-christ."

Why is it that the Amillennialist do not believe in a personal anti-christ that will be revealed at the time of the end? As we will see, the scriptures show in Daniel 7,8,9,10,11 and 12 that there will come an anti-christ in the latter days just before Jesus returns. The anti-christ is also mentioned in Revelation and as we have already seen, here in 2 Thessalonians 2:3 and in Matthew 24:15. When Jesus speaks about this anti-christ in Matthew 24:15, He is pointing to these 6 chapters of Daniel, referring to "the abomination that maketh desolate," and the anti-christ blaspheming God in the new temple.

How could all these passages from scripture be interpreted as a "sacrilege" in the Herodian temple in 70AD as Vander Waal says in his book?

Contrary to his view, we will see in the next chapters from Daniel that they all point to the anti-christ blaspheming God in the new temple at the end time. Daniel 7:25, *"And he* (the anti-christ) *shall speak great words against the most High,"* (Jesus Christ) and to show, that this is mentioned for the end times, verse 26 says, *"But the judgment shall sit, and they shall take away his* (the anti-christ's) *dominion, to consume and to destroy it unto the end."* The anti-christ will be destroyed, as in 2 Thess. 2:8, *"Whom the Lord shall consume with the spirit of His mouth, and shall destroy with the brightness of His coming."* It should be very clear here, that the anti-christ will be destroyed with "the brightness of His coming," after the return of Jesus, which shows that the anti-christ will be in the last days and has not been around from the beginning, and is not on earth presently, as the Amillennialist say. Dan. 8:11, *"Yea, he* (the anti-christ) *magnified himself, even to the prince of the host,* (Jesus) *and by him* (the anti-christ) *the daily sacrifice was taken away, and the place of his* (the anti-christ's) *sanctuary was cast down."* The anti-christ will take over the temple during the last 3 ½ years, as it says in verse 13, *"...How long shall be the vision concerning the daily sacrifice, and the transgression of desolation* (as in Matthew 24:15) *to give both the sanctuary and the host to be trodden under foot? 14. And he* (the angel) *said unto me, Unto two thousand and three hundred days; then shall the sanctuary be cleansed."* The angel says here that after the anti-christ has been removed from the temple, the temple will be cleansed for the coming of Jesus, to reign from His temple in Jerusalem. Again in Dan. 8:25, *"...He* (the anti-christ) *shall magnify himself in his heart... he shall also stand up against the Prince of princes; but he* (the anti-christ) *shall be broken without hand."* The anti-christ will be destroyed as in 2 Thess. 2:8, *"Whom the Lord shall consume with the spirit of His mouth, and shall destroy with the brightness of His coming."* Again Daniel shows that this is for the end times in Daniel 10:14, *"Now I* (the angel) *am come to make thee understand what shall befall thy people 'in the latter days:' for yet the vision is for many days."*

After everything we have read from Daniel so far, it is hard to believe that Amillennialist do not understand Daniel as foretelling the future. Vander Waal says that the Bible is not a book foretelling the future, and not a guide for the end time. But Daniel 10:14 clearly talks about the latter days. In Daniel 11:36 we read, *"And he* (the anti-christ) *shall exalt himself, and magnify himself above every god, and shall speak marvelous things against the God of gods and shall prosper till the indignation be accomplished: for that that is determined shall be done."* Again, in case we still did not believe that this points to the anti-christ in the future new temple, and not to the Herodian temple of 70 AD, note that here in Daniel is the same interpretation as in 2 Thess. 2:4 and Matthew 24:15. They all say the same thing: the anti-christ will blaspheme God in the temple until the indignation be accomplished, meaning the anti-christ will come to his end. (2 Thess. 2:8)

Daniel 11:31 says, *"And arms shall stand on his part* (Antiochus Epiphanes first, but later pointing to the anti-christ*), and they shall pollute the sanctuary of strength, and shall take away the daily sacrifice, and they shall place the abomination that maketh desolate"*. Since Antiochus Epiphanes did defile the Herodian temple in 168 BC, and erected a statue of Zeus in the temple, this defilement of the temple prefigured the abomination that Jesus predicted would occur in the end times in the new temple in Jerusalem by the anti-christ. This is the only place and time that Antiochus Epiphanies is interpreted, contrary to what the Amillennialist like Vander Waal say.

All other places point to the end time, when Jesus returns, as in Daniel 11:40, *"And at the time of the end, shall the king of the south* (Egypt and allies, as we will discuss later) *push at him* (the anti-christ)*: and the king of the North* (Russia) *shall come against him* (the anti-christ)... 41. He (the anti-christ) *shall enter also into the glorious land* (Israel)... *44. But tidings out of the east* (China and allies*) and out of the North* (second attack from Russia) *shall trouble him* (the anti-christ)...*45. And he* (the anti-christ) *shall plant the tabernacles of his* (this anti-christ) *palace between the seas in the glorious holy mountain* (Jerusalem)*; yet he* (the anti-christ) *shall come to his end, and none shall help him"* (the anti-christ). As we see from this passage in Daniel 11, the anti-christ will set up camp in Jerusalem during the last 3 ½ years of the tribulation when Russia, Egypt, China etc., come against him and he will come to his end, because there will be no one to help him. We have already seen what Paul says about him in 2 Thessalonians 2:8, *"whom the Lord shall destroy with the brightness of His coming."* If we're still not sure about interpreting Daniel literally, look at Daniel 12:1, *"and at that time* (continuing from Dan. 11 verse 45,) *shall Michael stand up, the great prince which standeth for the children of my people: and there shall be a time of trouble, such as never was, since there was a nation, even to that same time: and at that time thy people shall be delivered, everyone that shall be found written in the book."* Daniel says here, "a time of trouble, such as never was." Did Jesus not mention this in Matthew 24:21, *"For then shall be great tribulation, such as was not since the beginning of the world"?* And didn't the Amillennialist say that there has <u>always</u> been some sort of tribulation? Remember Rev. Verbrugge said, "The dispensationalist view of the rapture and the seven year tribulation and the plagues stirs up the imagination?" Seems to me that the Bible is very straightforward if taken literally, and it takes a vivid imagination to twist it around to mean anything other than a final tribulation period where the antichrist has his brief reign until Jesus returns to destroy him.

From this passage of Daniel 12, "and at that time shall Michael stand up...and at that time thy people shall be delivered, everyone one that shall be found written in the book", it should be clear that this passage points to the end time, when we will stand before God and the books are opened, and not something that has happened all the time on earth. How can we not take this seriously, but suggest that it "stirs up the imagination." How seriously should we take this tribulation? Look at Daniel 12:6, *"And one said to the man clothed in linen, which was upon the waters of the river,* (obviously an angel from God*), How long shall it be to the end of these wonders?"* and the angel replied in verse 7, *"... and sware by him that liveth for ever that it shall be for a time* (1 year) *times,* (2 years) *and a half;* (1/2 year) *and when he shall have accomplished to scatter the power of the holy people, all* *these things shall be finished."* The angel tells us it will be a total of 3 ½ years, the last three and one half years of the great tribulation of Matthew 24:15.

When the three and one half years are over, Jesus will return to start His reign for the 1000 year millennium and Satan will be bound for 1000 years. Dan. 12:11, *"And from the time that the daily sacrifice shall be taken away, and the abomination that maketh desolate set up, there shall be a thousand two hundred and ninety days."* Here again Daniel mentions the last three and one half years of the tribulation, when the anti-christ takes away the daily sacrifice, and starts the abomination that maketh desolate, as in Matthew 24:15.

Chapter 3

The Rapture
"After this...Come up hither"
Revelation 4:1

—ᗯᗯ—

R ev. Verbrugge says, "The rapture is unbiblical." How then do I read 2 Thessalonians 2:6-7, *"And now you know what withholdeth that he* (the anti-christ) *might be revealed in his time, 7. For the mystery of iniquity doth already work: only he who now letteth, will let, until he be taken out of the way."* I could never quite understand this verse, until I read the same verse in the New International Bible, where the same verse reads, "For the secret power of lawlessness is already at work; but the only one who now holds it back (the Holy Spirit) will continue to do so, until he is taken out of the way. (the rapture) 8. And then the lawless one (the anti-christ) will be revealed, whom the Lord Jesus will overthrow with the breath of his mouth and destroy by the splendor of his coming." Here the apostle Paul confirms what he already said in 2 Thess. 2:2, that the anti-christ will not be revealed until the rapture occurs, and that the anti-christ will come to his end, with the coming of Jesus Christ to the new earth. The anti-christ will not be revealed, until the Holy Spirit, who is restraining the anti-christ's appearing, is taken out of the way. As long as the church is on earth, the indwelling

Holy Spirit will continue to restrain the anti-christ. However, when the saints are raptured, the Holy Spirit will be taken out of the way, to allow Satan to bring forth the anti-christ. It is important to note however, that the Holy Spirit will not be removed from the earth completely, but will still convict the world of sin.

2 Thessalonians is not the only place in the Bible where we read about the rapture. Also, in 1 Corinthians 15:51, Paul talks about the rapture, as we read: *"Behold, I show you a mystery: We shall not all sleep, but we shall all be changed. 52. In a moment, in the twinkling of an eye, at the last trump: for the trumpet shall sound, and the dead shall be raised incorruptible, and we shall be changed."* Also 1 Thessalonians 4:14 talks about the rapture, when the apostle Paul says, *"For if we believe that Jesus died and rose again, even so them also which sleep in Jesus will God bring with Him. 15. For this we say unto you by the word of the Lord, that we which are alive and remain unto the coming of the Lord shall not prevent them which are asleep. 16. For the Lord Himself shall descend from heaven with a shout, with the voice of the archangel, and with the trump of God: and the dead in Christ shall rise first. 17. Then we which are alive and remain shall be caught up together with them in the clouds, to meet the Lord in the air: and so shall we ever be with the Lord. 18. Wherefore comfort ye one another with these words."*

Since the Amillennialist have such different opinions about the rapture, I doubt if we are much comfort to one another, because most Amillennialist do not believe in the rapture. Rev. Verbrugge said, "The rapture is unbiblical," which could be interpreted to mean no rapture at all. Others believe, like Rev. Hoekema says in CRC Viewpoint, "Amillennialist, therefore, believe in the rapture, but we believe that after this joyous meeting in the air, raised and transformed believers will go back with Christ to the earth." Hoekema continues with, "The second coming of Christ will be a single event. Amillennialist find no scriptural basis for the dispensationalist division of a second coming into two phases, with a seven-year period in between." We will deal with the seven year period later in a separate chapter.

The rapture is also referred to in Revelation 4:1, *"After this,* (after John had finished writing his letters to the churches), *I looked, and, behold, a door was opened in heaven: and the first voice which I heard was as it were a trumpet talking with me; which said, Come up hither."* Does this not point to the rapture, "Come up hither"? After this verse, the churches are not mentioned again in the Bible. They are noticeably absent. Then in verse 2, *"Immediately I was in the spirit; and, behold, a throne was set in heaven",* indicating that Jesus will meet his raptured saints in the air, and then return with them to heaven.

Before God punished the world with the flood, he removed Noah and his family of believers, and spared them from his judgment. (Genesis 6,7) Likewise, Lot was spared with his two daughters, for their faithfulness, and they were delivered from God's wrath on Sodom and Gomorah. (Genesis 9) Here already in the first book of the Bible, God is making references to the rapture. In Genesis 19:22 God says to Lot before he rains fire and brimstone on the wicked, *"Haste thee, escape thither; for I cannot do anything till thou come thither."* Similarly, the tribulation period, the anti-christ, and God's judgments on a wicked world, will not happen until after the rapture of his believers.

2 Peter 2:5-9 speaks of the same thing. *"And (God) spared not the old world, but saved Noah the eighth person, a preacher of righteousness, bringing in the flood upon the world of the ungodly; 6. And turning the cities of Sodom and Gomorah into ashes condemned them with an overthrow, making them an ensample unto those that after should live ungodly; 7. And delivered just Lot, vexed with the filthy conversation of the wicked; 8. (For that righteous*

47

man dwelling among them, in seeing and hearing, vexed his righteous soul from day to day with their unlawful deeds;) 9. The Lord knoweth how to deliver the godly <u>out</u> of temptations, and to reserve the unjust unto the <u>day of judgment</u> to be punished."

Tell me again that the rapture is "unbiblical"!

Chapter 4

Nebuchadnezzar's dream:
Daniel 2:28

—ᴍᴍ—

R ev. Verbrugge says in his sermons about Revelation, "In Rev. 17:10 we read: 'And there are seven kings'." About these kings he says, "we should not try to put names to them. These kings are seven Caesars that have been in the past." However, the Bible does not say that these seven kings are seven Caesars, and he just gave them names anyway, as being seven Caesars. To understand this passage from Revelation, one should go back to the book of Daniel. These seven kings are seven empires, as explained in several chapters of Daniel, starting with the dream of Nebuchadnezzar in Daniel 2:28. Through Daniel, the Lord interprets Nebuchadnezzar's dream as being about the future empires of the world. The head of gold, being Nebuchadnezzar, king of the Babylonian Empire, which will be overtaken by the Medes and Persians, as in Daniel 5:31, *"and Darius the Mede, took the kingdom."* (from Nebuchadnezzar's son Belshazzar). Then the Greek Empire will take the Medo-Persian Empire, as in Daniel 10:20, *"the prince of Grecia shall come."* After that the two legs of the image in Nebuchadnezzar's dream, Rome, will overtake the Grecian empire, which happened almost 500 years after Daniel prophesied this to Nebuchadnezzar, we know from the book of Romans. Daniel 2:40 says, *"the fourth kingdom shall be strong as iron...42. And the toes of the feet were part of iron, and part of clay, so the kingdom shall be partly strong, and partly broken."* Daniel 2:44 says, *"And in the days of these kings* (10 kings) *shall the God of heaven set up a kingdom which shall never be destroyed."* This kingdom, which Daniel mentions here, must be in the future, because it says, "it shall never be destroyed." Since all kingdoms on earth, have either been destroyed or will be destroyed, before Jesus returns to the new earth to start his reign in the 1000 year Millennium, as He has promised all through the scriptures, it should be clear that this kingdom will be in the future.

Rev. Verbrugge says, "Revelation is not a book of the end times, not a book foretelling the future, and a good reformed does not make predictions about the end time, and the future." However, the Lord, through Daniel just did foretell the future here, when He told Nebuchadnezzar in Daniel 2:28, *"But there is a God in Heaven that revealeth secrets, and maketh known to the king Nebuchadnezzar what shall be in the latter days."* If God in His wisdom revealed to Nebuchadnezzar what will happen in the "latter days" (the future), should we not therefore believe this also, and take it literally, and not symbolically as representing seven Caesars? Daniel 2:44, *"...and the kingdom shall not be left to other people, but it shall break in pieces, and consume all these kingdoms, and it shall stand forever."* Forever makes it clear, that this kingdom is for the future and therefore so much for reasoning that the Bible does not foretell the future. Even King Nebuchadnezzar believed that God predicted the future, when he said in Daniel 2:47, *"The king answered unto Daniel, and said, Of a truth it is, that your God is a God of god's and a Lord of kings, and a revealer of secrets, seeing that thou couldest reveal this secret."* Here even Nebuchadnezzar admits that all the predictions

God revealed through Daniel are true, and not symbolic, as some who know God's word so well are inclined to say. No wonder 2 Peter 1:19 says, *"We have also a more sure word of prophecy; whereunto ye do well to take heed,* (to take it seriously)...*20. Knowing this first, that, no prophecy of the scripture is of any private interpretation. 21. For prophecy came not in old time by the will of man, but Holy men of God spake as they were moved by the Holy Ghost."*

Daniel 2:44, *"And in the days of these kings, shall the God of heaven set up a kingdom which shall never be destroyed:"* What is this kingdom that shall never be destroyed? Jesus mentions this kingdom in His prayer, when He says, "Our Father who art in heaven, Hallowed be Thy Name. Thy kingdom come, Thy will be done on earth as it is in heaven." Jesus mentions here a kingdom, which is yet to come, because he says, "Thy kingdom come." It has not yet arrived. And furthermore, He says, "Thy will be done on earth as it is in heaven." His will, will never be done on earth as in heaven, until Jesus returns to make a new earth, "where righteousness dwelleth."

So Jesus, in His prayer, also points to this new earth which will never be destroyed, the same kingdom spoken of in Daniel 2:44. One might ask why it is important to know all this? My answer would be; if the Lord found it necessary to tell king Nebuchadnezzar about the future and what will happen in the end time, the Lord must have wanted us to know also, so that we can understand Revelation better, including Revelation 17:10. This is the passage where Rev. Verbrugge interpreted the "seven kings" as seven Caesars. Rev. 17:10 says further, *"five are fallen* (Assyria, Egypt, Babylon, Medo-Persia, Greece), *one is* (Rome, at the time John wrote Revelation in 63 AD on Patmos*) and the other is not yet come, and when he cometh, he must continue a short space."* Five are fallen, are the first five world empires from history: Assyria, Egypt, Babylon, Medo-Persia, and

Greece, all included in Nebuchadnezzar's dream. All these empires had come and gone already at the time John wrote Revelation on Patmos. Rome was still in power then, The Roman Empire. The other is not yet come, the seventh king, or empire from Rev. 17:10, "and there are seven kings." This seventh king is mentioned in Dan. 2:42 as well as in Rev. 17:12. It will be the last kingdom on earth, before Jesus will establish the kingdom of Daniel 2:44; *"And in the time of these kings, shall the God of heaven set up a kingdom which shall never be destroyed."*

Revelation 17:12 points to the ten toes of Daniel 2:44. Revelation 17:12 says: *"and the 10 horns, which thou sawest, are 10 kings which have received no kingdom as yet, but receive power as kings one hour with the beast"* (the anti-christ). Here in Rev. 17:12, the apostle John talks about the 10 horns being 10 kings, the same as the 10 toes from Daniel 2:44. These 10 kings will form a revised Roman empire in the last days, as the 10 toes of Nebuchadnezzar's dream emerging from the two legs of iron, the Roman Empire.

Revelation 17:11, *"And the beast that was, and is not, even he is the eighth, and is of the seven and goeth into perdition."* This refers to the seventh kingdom, specifically the Roman Empire, which was, but is no longer. However, the Roman Empire was never replaced by another world empire. It will again come to power as the eighth world kingdom under the anti-christ, but is actually still part of the seventh. "Into perdition" is also referred to in 2 Thessalonians 2:3, *"and that man of sin be revealed, the son of perdition;"* Then we go on with 2 Thessalonians 2:8, *"and then shall that Wicked be revealed,* (the anti-christ) *whom the Lord shall consume with spirit of His mouth, and shall destroy with the brightness of His coming:"*

This verse 11, from Revelation 17, "the beast that was, and is not," is about the anti-christ, who will reign as the "eighth" with the seven kings during this last empire on earth, before he (the anti-christ) will go into perdition. Then Jesus returns to set up His "kingdom which shall never be destroyed." If we still would not believe, after reading Daniel 2 and Rev. 17, that these passages point to the seven world empires, and that the seventh empire becomes the final future empire when the anti-christ will be revealed, and be in control of the whole world as in 2 Thessalonians 2:3, then, well, there is still more proof in scripture.

Daniel 7:23. *"Thus he said, The fourth beast shall be the fourth kingdom upon the earth... 24. And the ten horns out of this kingdom are ten kings that shall arise; and he shall be diverse from the first... 25. And he shall speak great words against the most High."* Here, the Lord instructs Daniel to prophesy about the vision of the four beasts (four empires), where he said: *"the fourth beast shall be the fourth kingdom upon the earth"* (as in Nebuchadnezzar's dream). When Daniel wrote the book of Daniel, during the Babylonian Empire, the Assyrian, and the Egyptian Empires had already been and fallen. The Medo-Persian and Grecian Empires had to come yet, before the Roman Empire would come to power. From Daniel's perspective, this makes the Roman Empire the fourth kingdom. When John wrote Revelation on Patmos, and said: "Five are fallen" he was referring to Assyria, Egypt, Babylon, Medo-Persia, Greece. The one that 'was' for John was Rome, and the one that was to come was a revised Roman empire. From John's perspective, the seventh kingdom. We can see clearly that Daniel and John were both speaking about the same kingdom from which the anti-christ would arise. And for each of them, this kingdom was yet in the future.

Rev. 17:11, *"And the beast that was, and is not, even he is the eighth, and is of the seven, and goeth into perdition."* If not taken literally, in comparison with the book of Daniel, this passage from Revelation is difficult to interpret. It should be clear by reading them both that they are pointing specifically to the anti-christ. How can anyone after all this, still believe that this points to Antiochus Epiphanes? Daniel continues to make it clear that this is still in the future in Dan. 7:26, *"But judgment shall sit, and they shall take away his* (the anti-christ's) *dominion to consume and to destroy it to the end,"*

If we would still not be sure that all these prophecies from Daniel point to the end times: to the future empire of the last days, see Dan. 8:16, *"Gabriel* (the angel), *make this man to understand the vision."* And, in verse 17, *"He* (the angel) *said unto me, understand O son of man, for the time appointed the end shall be."* It is no wonder we do not understand Revelation, if we do not take Daniel literally. God wants us to understand His word. The Bible was not written to confuse us, as it is written in here in Daniel, *"Understand, O son of man,"* and again in verse 19, *"and he* (the angel) *said, behold, I will make thee know what shall be in the last end of the indignation, for the time appointed the end shall be."* What a strange concept to believe that God, in His perfect wisdom, would give His children His Word, but that His words would mean something other than what was written. He wants us to understand. He wants us to take His Word literally.

Still need more proof? Read Daniel chapter 8: 9-10, 24-25, chapter 9:27, and chapter 11: 40-46. It is difficult to believe, that Amillennialist do not believe that Daniel is talking here about the future, the time of the end, the latter days, just before Jesus returns.

Rev. Vander Waal has this to say about the end time, "Misconceptions about Bible prophecy lead to misunderstanding in the area of Exegesis. When Daniel 12 talks about the 'time of the end' (verses 4 and 9) some translations and interpretations turn this into the 'end time'. This in turn fosters the notion that Daniel's visions deal with the absolute end of History, thus his prophecies are not read as pointing to the events of Antiochus Epiphanes, who ruled 175 – 164 BC but as portraying events at the very end of time. The expression 'the last days', which is used by other prophets, has furthered the same misconceptions."

In spite of everything we have read in Daniel, including the angel Gabriel saying, *"Understand, O son of man ...for the time appointed the end shall be"*, here Vander Waal says, "this is a misconception, it all points to Antiochus Epiphanes 175-164 BC...Also, his expression, 'the last days', which is used by some of the other prophets, has furthered the same misconceptions." It does make one think, because indeed all prophets do make it clear that when they talked about "the last days," they also mentioned that this points to the time when Jesus returns, "the absolute end of history" as Vander Waal puts it.

Rev. Verbrugge has this to say about the end time, "The dispensationalist's view of the rapture and the seven year tribulation and the plagues, stirs up the imagination, does not hold up to the creationist view." If we still think that the tribulation stirs the imagination, and that the tribulation will not be something terrible in the future, as Jesus said in Matthew 24:21, and if we still want to take the empires as being symbolic, read Daniel 8:20, *"The ram which thou sawest, having two horns are the kings of Media and Persia.* (from Nebuchadnezzar's dream, being the 4th, empire) *21. And the rough goat is the king of Grecia:* (the 5th empire of Nebuchadnezzar's dream) *and the great horn that is between his eyes is the first king.* (Alexander the Great) *22... four kingdoms shall stand up out of the nation* (Alexander's four generals Ptolemy, Seleucus, Cassander, and Lysimachus, who divide the empire) *23. And in the latter time of their kingdom, when the transgressors are come to the full, a king of fierce countenance and understanding dark sentences shall stand up. 24. And his power shall be mighty...and shall destroy the mighty and the holy people. 25...and he shall magnify himself...* (same as in 2 Thess. 2:4 and Dan. 11:36)...*he shall also stand up against the Prince of Princes* (Jesus Christ)*, but he shall be broken without hands.*" This passage points to Antiochus Epiphanes, ruler of Syria 175-163 BC who conquered Jerusalem, raised a statue in the temple and defiled it.

Daniel's prophecies were not in any way symbolic, but happened exactly as foretold. Therefore the rest of his prophecies are not symbolic either. Daniel said a king from the fourth empire would take Jerusalem and defile the temple, and it happened. When Daniel also predicts the same thing will happen by a ruler of the eighth kingdom, only much, much worse, we can believe that he means this literally! In Daniel chapter 12, where he speaks of this king at the time of the end, he is speaking about the anti-christ, in no uncertain terms. Antiochus Epiphanes foreshadows the anti-christ and the certainty of his personal appearance in the latter days. It also assures us that when Jesus returns, the anti-christ will come to his end.

Chapter 5

Daniel's 69 Weeks

—ᄿᄿᄿ—

As if the Lord knew that we would have difficulty believing that these prophecies are to be taken literally, the Lord instructs Daniel to prophesy more about the future in Daniel 9. Here Daniel remembers Jeremiah's prophecies in Jeremiah 25:11-12, *"and this whole land shall be a desolation, and an astonishment; and these nations shall serve the king of Babylon seventy years, 12. And it shall come to pass, when 70 years are accomplished, that I will punish the king of Babylon, and that nation, saith the Lord..."*

Before the Jews were even taken to Babylon by Nebuchadnezzar, Jeremiah already prophesied that they would only be there 70 years, and then the Lord would have compassion, and let them go back to their own land. Is this not foretelling the future by the Lord Himself through Jeremiah the prophet? Daniel knew that these 70 years were almost finished, and Daniel asks the Lord about Jerusalem and the sanctuary (the temple which was destroyed by Nebuchadnezzar). Daniel 9:21, *"Yea, whiles I was speaking in prayer, even ... Gabriel (the angel) ... touched me... 20. And informed me, and talked with me, and said, O Daniel, I am come forth to give thee skill and understanding. 23... therefore understand the matter, and consider the vision. 24.*

s are determined upon thy people and upon thy
nish the transgression, and to make an end of
ake reconciliation for iniquity, and to bring
_rtasting righteousness, and seal up the vision and
prophecy, and to anoint the most Holy. (Jesus Christ) *25.*
Know therefore and understand, that from the going forth
of the commandment to restore and to build Jerusalem unto
the Messiah the Prince shall be seven weeks, and threescore
and two weeks: the street shall be built again, and the wall,
even in troublous times. 26. And after threescore and two
weeks shall Messiah (Jesus) *be cut off* (crucified) *but not for*
himself: and the people of the prince that shall come, shall
destroy the city (Jerusalem) *and the sanctuary;* (the Temple)
and the end thereof shall be with a flood; and unto the end of
the war, desolations are determined."

Daniel again speaks about the desolations. This was also spoken of by Jesus in Matthew 24:15, and 2 Thessalonians 2:4. Daniel says that from the time of the commandment to start building Jerusalem, until the time that Jesus will be crucified will be 69 weeks, as we will see later.

In Nehemiah 2:5, Nehemiah talks about what just has been mentioned in Dan. 9:21-25, and said, *"...If it please the king* (Artaxerxes)*...that thou wouldest send me to Judah, unto the city of my fathers sepulchers, that I may build it. 6...so it pleased the king to send me."* Here Artaxerxes, King of Persia, gives Nehemiah permission to go to Jerusalem and rebuild the walls of the city, exactly as the prophet Jeremiah had prophesied 70 years earlier. The Medes and Persians had taken over the Babylonian empire, just as Daniel had prophesied, so Nehemiah now served with the Persians. Ezra had already left earlier to start rebuilding the temple in Jerusalem, (Ezra 3:8). This Bible passage of Nehemiah 2:5, where the king Artaxerxes gives Nehemiah permission to go to Jerusalem to build the city, has been recorded in history as happening in 445 BC. While many Christians label most of this as symbolic, and therefore do not take this literally, non-Christian historians take this passage from the Bible quite literally as the truth, and have recorded it as such. One can look this up in most libraries. Daniel 9:25, *"Know therefore and understand."* The Lord wants us to understand what Daniel is saying here. *"Know therefore and understand that...seventy weeks are determined."*

What is a week? In Genesis 29:27 we read, *"Fulfill her week, and we will give thee this also for the service which thou shalt serve with me yet seven other years...30...and served him yet seven other years."* It is clear from this passage of scripture, that in the Old Testament, often a week represented 7 years. A month was always exactly 30 days, as in Genesis 7:11, *"In the six hundredth year of Noah's life, in the second month on the seventeenth day of the month, the same day were all the fountains of the great deep broken up."* Genesis 8:4, *"And the arc rested in the seventh month, on the seventeenth day of the month upon the mountains of Ararat."* The flood lasted from the seventeenth day of the second month, until the seventeenth day of the seventh month. Exactly 5 months, and since Genesis 7:24 says, *"And the water prevailed upon the earth an hundred and fifty days,"* it means that a month was exactly 30 days in biblical times.

Now that we know that a week means 7 years, and a month had exactly 30 days, it is easier to understand Daniel 9:25, "seven weeks and threescore and two weeks," for a total of 69 weeks, times 7 years is 483 years altogether. Therefore from the time that Artaxerxes gave Nehemiah permission to start rebuilding Jerusalem, until Jesus entered Jerusalem through the Eastern Gate on Palm Sunday to be crucified, is 483 years, as in Daniel 9:26, *"Shall Messiah be cut off"* (be crucified).

Daniel 9:26, *"And the people of the prince that shall come,"* (the anti-christ) *shall destroy the city* (Jerusalem) *and the sanctuary* (the Holy Temple)." This happened in 70

AD, when the Romans destroyed Jerusalem and the temple. Daniel says here that Jerusalem and the sanctuary will be destroyed by the people of the prince that shall come (the anti-christ). Notice also, that Daniel says here the anti-christ will come from the people that destroyed Jerusalem. Since Jerusalem was destroyed by the Romans, the anti-christ will therefore come from the countries that were occupied by the Romans. This will be the revised Roman Empire, the 10 toes from Dan. 2:42, as well as the ten horns from Rev. 17:12, being the 7th empire from Nebuchadnezzar's dream. Is it not amazing that if one takes the Bible literally how everything falls into place?

Notice that Jeremiah prophesied 70 years would pass before the people of Israel could return to Jerusalem. It was literal and was fulfilled exactly as prophesied. Daniel is well aware of this as he prophesies 70 weeks of years. (70 times 7 years) He breaks it up however into 7 weeks and 62 weeks until the Messiah is cut off. Again, this was literal and was fulfilled exactly in 483 years when Jesus was crucified. Does it not stand to reason then, that the rest of these prophecies are to be taken literally as well?

Chapter 6

Daniel's 70ᵗʰ week

—ɯ—

So far only 69 weeks of the 70 weeks of Daniel have been mentioned. Dan. 9:27 says, *"and he* (the anti-christ) *shall confirm the covenant with many* (many nations) *for one week:* (7 years as in Genesis 29:27), *and in the midst of the week* (3 ½ years) *he* (the anti-christ) *shall cause the sacrifice and the oblation to cease, and for the overspreading of abominations, he* (the anti-christ) *shall make it desolate,"* same again as in 2 Thess. 2:4. Here in Daniel 9:27, Daniel talks about the one week (7 year) tribulation period, just before Jesus returns, when the anti-christ will make a covenant with many nations, and for the first 3 ½ years, there will be peace. However, after 3 ½ years, in the middle of this 7 year covenant, he (the anti-christ) will break the covenant, when he (the anti-christ) "shall cause the overspreading of abominations that maketh desolate."

This is what the apostle Paul described in 2 Thess. 2:4 as well as what Jesus is talking about in Matthew 24:15, when he says, *"When you therefore shall see the abomination of desolation spoken of by Daniel the prophet, standing in the Holy place."* (the new temple in Jerusalem). Jesus here is pointing to what will happen in the future, as prophesied also by Daniel in Dan. 9:27.

Vander Waal has this interpretation of Daniel 9:27, "In Daniel 9 we read, that Daniel was studying the book of Jeremiah, which contained a promise that Jerusalem would be restored after 70 years. Because this promise had not yet been fulfilled, Daniel prayed to the Lord about Jerusalem's plight. After this prayer, Daniel was told by the angel Gabriel that the 70 years are 'seventy weeks of years'. Thus is would be much longer than Daniel expected before the glorious restoration came about."

However, Gabriel did not say that it would take seventy weeks of years to finish the restoration of Jerusalem. Instead Gabriel said it would take 'seventy weeks' to seal up the vision and prophecy, ... and to anoint the Most Holy (Jesus Christ). Gabriel also said that it would take 69 weeks of years until Jesus was crucified. Daniel 9:25, "Know therefore, and understand, that from the going forth of the commandment to restore and to build Jerusalem unto 'the Messiah the Prince (Jesus Christ) shall be seven weeks, and threescore and two weeks." Gabriel therefore said it would take 69 weeks not 70 weeks. It would take the first seven weeks (49 years) "for the street to be built again and the wall, even in troublous times. 26. And after threescore and two weeks, shall Messiah be cut off," (be crucified). Daniel says here, that Jesus will be crucified 69 weeks (of years), from the time the commandment was given to restore and rebuild Jerusalem.

Vander Waal continues with, "The return to Jerusalem and the initial restoration of the services in the temple would take seven 'weeks'." Since Gabriel said that the restoration would be finished in 69 weeks (seven weeks, and threescore and two weeks), where do the other seven weeks come from?

Vander Waal then says, "After that, the reconstruction of Jerusalem would continue, but it would be in a troubled time. After the sixty-second week, an anointed one would be cut off. This is a reference to the temporary interruption in the legitimate priestly service during the days of Antiochus Epiphanes."

I will never understand, how Jesus Christ could have been replaced by Antiochus Epiphanes, as Vander Waal says, "an anointed one" (Jesus Christ) will be "cut off." This is a reference to "Antiochus Epiphanes."

First of all, when Vander Waal says, "an anointed one would be cut off," he combined two totally different events into one; like Messiah shall be cut off (crucified), and an "anointed one" (as in after seventy weeks to anoint the most Holy) when Jesus returns, to set up His millennium kingdom on earth when He will be anointed.

The first event has happened, when Jesus was crucified; the second event, the return of Jesus, "to anoint the most Holy," of course has not happened yet.

Vander Waal continues with, "Daniel 9 speaks of a strange people destroying the city and the sanctuary, with their tyranny lasting one 'week'. Halfway through that 'week' the sacrifices and the offerings would be halted." Fortunately, Rev. Hoekema has a different view. In CRC Viewpoint he says, "The two stage coming is not in harmony with the scriptures. The dispensationalist believe their doctrine of a 7 year time interval, between the rapture and the final second coming, on a misinterpretation of Daniel 9:24-27. According to this passage, sixty-nine sevens (seven year periods) is the time span between the command to rebuild Jerusalem, and the coming of the anointed one that is the 'Messiah.' So far so good." Here Rev. Hoekema says, "so far so good": in other words, the Amillennialist do believe Daniel up to here. It is little wonder they have so much trouble interpreting the Bible, when they mix up the words so badly. Nowhere did Daniel say, "sixty-nine sevens (seven year periods) is the time span between the command to rebuild Jerusalem, and the coming of the anointed one that is the 'Messiah'!" He never said that at all. Hoekema has totally confused the 70 weeks and the 69 weeks.

However, Hoekema continues with; "But then the dispensationalists insist that Daniel's seventieth week, 'seven' (or seven year period) described in verse 27, has not yet occurred and will not occur until the time of Christ's second coming. It is however not warranted to assume that a period of over nineteen hundred years must elapse between the fulfillment of the last part of Daniel's prophecy. Daniel's seventieth 'seven' (or 'week' of years), as a matter of fact, has already been fulfilled at the time of Christ's first coming, when He was put to death. We interpret 'the anointed one will be cut off' (vs. 26), and 'he will put an end to sacrifice and offerings' (vs. 27), as referring to Christ's death."

Rev. Hoekema says here, "We interpret 'the anointed one will cut be off' (vs. 26), and 'he will put an end to sacrifice and offerings' (vs. 27) as referring to Christ's death." Where does Rev. Hoekema read in Daniel 9:26, "The anointed one will be cut off"? What Daniel really says in Daniel 9:26 is, *"After threescore and two weeks shall <u>Messiah</u> be cut off"* (Jesus crucified). Daniel does not say, "The anointed one will be cut off." Daniel's reference to "anointing the most Holy" is in a different verse and in a different context.

The "anointing" and " being cut off" are two totally different events!

Dan 9:26 says, *"And after threescore and two weeks shall Messiah be cut off."* This refers specifically to Jesus being crucified, which happened almost 2000 years ago. Daniel 9:24 says, *"Seventy weeks are determined ... to finish the transgression, and to make an end of sins, to make reconciliation for iniquity ... to seal up the vision ... and to anoint the most Holy."* Note that "making an end of sins" comes way before the "anointing of the most Holy." The end of sins has not happened yet; nor has the anointing of the most Holy. It should be obvious therefore, that there is already a gap of almost 2000 years between Messiah being cut off, and the anointing of the most Holy. Why do we have such difficulties with interpreting the Bible literally, as in Dan.9:24? *"Seventy weeks are determined ... to bring in everlasting righteousness... and to anoint the most Holy."* We will not have "everlasting righteousness" until Jesus returns to the new earth. The anointing of the most Holy has to be in the future, when Jesus returns, and does not agree with Vander Waal's statement, "the two verses 26 and 27 are talking about the same period, the age of Antiochus Epiphanes."

This is most unlikely, because Antiochus Epiphanes ruled Syria from 175-164 BC, and during that time he defiled the Herodian temple, by erecting a statue of Zeus in this temple, he sacrificed swine upon the altar, and he encouraged his soldiers to commit fornication in the temple.

The defilement of the temple that Jesus predicted in Matthew 24:15, had not happened yet (obviously), but would occur at the end time, as also seen in Luke 21:20. When the apostle Paul wrote 2 Thessalonians 2:1-5 in 51-52 AD, Antiochus Epiphanes had already died over 200 years earlier. Paul is speaking about the anti-christ, *"that man of sin... the son of perdition; 4. Who opposeth and exhalteth himself above all that is called God, or that is worshipped; so that he as God sitteth in the temple of God, shewing himself that he is God."* Paul says in 2 Thess. 2:5, *"Remember ye not, that, when I was yet with you, I told you these things?"* Paul is referring to Jesus' words in Matthew 24:15, *"When you therefore shall see the abomination of desolation, spoken of by Daniel the prophet, stand in the holy place* (the new temple in Jerusalem) *(whoso readeth, let him understand)."*

Jesus makes it clear, that He expects us to understand what He is talking about here, that we take this literally, and not symbolically. Jesus and Daniel and Paul were all speaking about the same thing. Isn't it amazing how the Bible confirms itself, that everything is true? If we didn't believe it was to be taken literally, we would surely have a problem with the number of times it says the same thing, and the number of authors that confirm each other.

Daniel 9:27 says, *"In the midst of the week* (seven years), *he* (the anti-christ) *shall cause the sacrifice and the oblation to cease."* In the middle of the 7 years, or, after 3 ½ years.

Daniel 12:11 says the same thing, *"And from the time that the daily sacrifice shall be taken away, and the abomination that maketh desolate set up,* (the anti-christ blaspheming God in the new temple in Jerusalem), *there shall be a thousand two hundred and ninety days."* Again, as in Daniel 9:27, a period of 3 ½ weeks.

Also Daniel 12:6 says, *"How long shall it be to the end of these wonders? 7... it shall be for a time* (1 year), *times* (2 years), *and an half time* (half a year),*"* again for a total of 3 ½ years. We know, that this is for the end times as in Dan. 12:7, *"all these things shall be finished."* It is so much easier to understand when one takes the Bible literally, because then these passages confirm each another, i.e. that the anti-christ will blaspheme God in the new temple to be built yet before Jesus returns.

If this is still not convincing, read Daniel 11:36-45, *"and he* (the anti-christ) *shall exalt himself, and magnify himself above every god...40. And at the time of the end shall the king of the south* (Egypt and allies) *push at him* (the anti-christ*): and the king of the north* (Russia) *shall come against him* (the anti-christ) *... 41. He* (the anti-christ) *shall enter also into the glorious land* (Israel) *... 44.* But tidings out of the east, (as in Rev. 16:12) and out of the north (second attack from Russia) *shall trouble him... 45. And he* (the anti-christ*) shall plant the tabernacles of his palace between the seas in the glorious holy mountain* (Jerusalem) *yet he* (the anti-christ) *shall come to his end, and none shall help him."*

This passage tells us that the anti-christ will be attacked from all sides, and will temporarily set up camp in Jerusalem, but will be destroyed in the end as in 2 Thess. 2:8, *"Whom the Lord shall consume with the spirit of His mouth, and shall destroy with the brightness of His coming."*

Chapter 7

"Remember Abraham, Isaac, and Israel...all this land that I have spoken of will I give unto your seed and they shall inherit it forever." Exodus 32:13

—୰—

Reverend Verbrugge says, "Revelation is not a book for the future. Not a prewritten history." However, as we have just seen from the book of Daniel, Daniel gave us many prophesies; truly a "prewritten history," as the Lord told him to write about those visions for the future. There are many places, where the Lord foretells the future, as in Deuteronomy 30, where the Lord tells Moses the future for the people of Israel.

Although they had not yet crossed the river Jordan to the Promised Land, the Lord promised that they would. God told Moses, that they would later forsake the Lord, and therefore would be punished, and scattered all through the nations amongst the heathen. This happened in part when Nebuchadnezzar took the Jews to Babylon in 586 BC, and again later in AD 70 with the destruction of Jerusalem, when the Jews were scattered all through the nations just as the Lord had told Moses thousands of years earlier.

However, the Lord also promises here in Deuteronomy 30, thousands of years before it happened, that the Jews would come back again into their own country. On May 14, 1948, for the first time since Nebuchadnezzar took the Jews out of their country to Babylon, the Jews once again had control of their own land, just as the Lord had promised. The United Nations officially proclaimed that the land of Palestine again belonged in Israeli hands, and the State of Israel declared its Independence. Deuteronomy 30:8 says, *"And thou shalt return, and obey the voice of the Lord."* It does not seem that Israel today is obeying the voice of the Lord yet; however they will when Jesus comes back to the new earth, when they will inherit Israel forever.

Not only in Deuteronomy, but also in almost every other book of the Bible, do we find prophecies that the Jews will come back to their own country, and will inherit it forever. We have discussed previously, from many different verses, that after the people of Israel have been scattered all through the nations, they will finally return to their homeland. This is exactly what happened May 14, 1948. We have also determined that this would be a sign that Jesus would soon return.

The apostle Peter says in 2 Peter 1:19, *"We have also a more sure word of prophecy; whereunto ye do well that ye take heed,* (take it seriously) *... 20. Knowing this first, that no prophecy of the scripture is of any private interpretation. 21. For the prophecy came not in old time by the will of man: but holy men of God spake, as they were moved by the Holy Ghost."*

Jeremiah also prophesied that the Jews would come back in Jeremiah 23:3, *"And I will gather the remnant of my flock out of all countries whither I have driven them, and I will bring them again to their folds; and they shall be fruitful and increase ... and they shall fear no more, nor be dismayed, neither shall they be lacking, saith the Lord. 5. Behold, the days come, saith the Lord, that I will raise unto David a righteous Branch*

(Jesus) *and a King* (Jesus) *shall reign and prosper, and shall execute judgment and justice in the earth."*

In verse 3 Jeremiah says, "and I will bring them again to their folds," and in verse 4, "they shall fear no more, neither shall they be lacking." It should be clear from this, that Jeremiah is talking here about the new earth, as in Jeremiah 23:6, *"In his days Judah shall be saved, and Israel shall dwell safely: and this is the name whereby he shall be called: THE LORD OUR RIGHTEOUSNESS."*

When we talked about Daniel 9 we found that verses 26 and 27 could not be referring to the same time, because it says seventy weeks are determined to ... bring in "everlasting righteousness," which points to the return of Jesus to the new earth. Here Jeremiah makes it clear, that he is talking about the new earth, when he says, "Israel shall dwell in safety" and also his reference to "The Lord our Righteousness" just as in Daniel 9.

Jeremiah 23:7, *"Therefore, behold, the days come, saith the Lord, that they shall no more say, The Lord liveth, which brought up the children of Israel out of the land of Egypt; 8. But the Lord liveth, which brought up and which led the seed of the house of Israel out of the North country* (Russia, as we will deal with later), *and from the countries whither I had driven them; and they shall dwell in their own land."*

The Lord could not have made it any clearer than what He said here in Jeremiah, that the Jews will come back to their country, and will stay there forever as God's chosen people. Jeremiah 30:3 says, *"For, lo, the days come, saith the Lord, that I will bring again the captivity of my people Israel and Judah, saith the Lord: and I will cause them to return to the land that I gave to their fathers and they shall posses it."*

How can anyone not believe that this prophecy was fulfilled on May 14, 1948 when for the first time since Nebuchadnezzar took the Jews to Babylon, the Jews had their own state of Israel back again, and as the prophets have said all through God's word, they will inherit Israel forever, as God's chosen people.

How can Vander Waal say, "Jesus shows how the Lord finally dismisses Jerusalem, the city that slaughtered the lamb? Henceforth, He will no longer recognize the Jews as His chosen people." (He died for all of us, not just the Jews)

Rev. Hoekema in CRC Viewpoint says, "Dispensationalists often appeal to Romans 11 to support their view on Israel. Remember however, that even if we were inclined to understand verses 25-26 as teaching a future national conversion of Israel, we would still have to admit, that Romans 11 says nothing about a regathering of Israel to their homeland, or about a future role of Christ over a Millennium Israelite kingdom." (However all the prophets actually do tell us about the regathering of Israel to their homeland, as we will see later.)

Hoekema continues with, "Then how can Paul be teaching us that God has a separate purpose for the Jews, and a separate future for Israel?" It should be clear from Romans 11:26-27 that the Lord has forgiven the Jews, and that they will be His chosen people forever, as in Romans 11:26, *"And so shall all Israel be saved: as it is written, There shall come out of Zion the Deliverer, and shall turn away all ungodliness from Jacob:"*

Remember, it says in Genesis 35:10, *"And God said unto him, Thy name is Jacob, thy name shall not be called any more Jacob, but Israel shall be thy name and He called his name Israel."* Since the Lord Himself changed the name of Jacob into Israel, we could read Romans 11:26 as, *"There shall come out of Zion the Deliverer, and shall turn away all ungodliness from Israel:"* It can hardly be interpreted, as Vander Waal says, "He (God) will no longer recognize the Jews as His chosen people." Instead it shows that the Lord did not dismiss the Jews as His chosen people, but will keep His covenant with Israel forever.

Vander Waal says, "The dispensationalists make the kingdom of heaven into a Jewish kingdom that shall arise after Christ's return... What we face here is more then irresponsible reading of the texts... Dispensationalists want to read the scriptures literally, therefore the unfulfilled prophecies must be fulfilled in the kingdom of heaven, and take on an earthly form, as in Luke 1:32-33, that Jesus be given the throne of His father David, and that he will be their king over the house of Jacob forever in the kingdom of heaven. But how is this interpretation to be harmonized with the assurance that there will be no end to his kingdom; that we are not told."

There is nothing to tell other then to take Luke 1:32-33 literally, as Jesus said here. That Jesus will be given the throne of His father David: and that He will be King over the house of Jacob (Israel) for ever; and of His kingdom there shall be no end, just as the Bible says.

Why can we not take all this literally, as the Bible says it will be? Like in 2 Peter 1:19, *"We have a more sure word of prophecy."*

Vander Waal also says, "When Paul talks about Jesus king, he isn't referring to a kingship over the church, plus a kingship over the house of Jacob. Jesus is king of the church, and the church is the house of Jacob." As we have just seen, the Lord changed the name of Jacob into Israel. Shall we therefore read, "the church is the house of Israel?" The Bible does not say this at all.

Vander Waal continues with, "Reading the Bible and singing psalms would be difficult, if it were governed by the distorted dispensationalist understanding of the covenant, church, and kingdom. We would then have to think of the contemporary state of Israel and the Jews as a race, whenever we read or sang about the people of Israel, the house of Jacob, or the descendants of Abraham. He (Lindsey) is in conflict with the confessions of the reformation, which do not teach that the Jewish people and the city of Jerusalem will be dominant at the end of time." Where does the Bible teach that the Jews and the city of Jerusalem will not be dominant at the time of the end?

This is a clear example of "Replacement Theology" where church doctrine attempts to change the literal and historical promises God made to His chosen people of Israel, and reassigns them to the church. This theology is a perversion of scripture. God's promises are very specific between the people of Israel and the Gentiles. When God refers to the people of Israel (Jacob) He often refers to the "seed" of Abraham, thereby signifying a physical lineage. There is no symbolism here.

Genesis 17:7-8, *"and I will establish my covenant between me and thee and thy seed after thee in their generations for an everlasting covenant to be a God unto thee, and to thy seed after thee, 8. And I will give unto thee and to thy seed after thee, the land wherein thou art a stranger, all the land of Canaan, for an everlasting possession, and I will be their God."*

Zechariah 12:2 says, *"Behold, I will make Jerusalem a cup of trembling... 3. And in that day will I make Jerusalem a burdensome stone for all people..."* Luke 21:24 says, *"Jerusalem shall be trodden down of the Gentiles until the times of the Gentiles be fulfilled."* The times of the gentiles were fulfilled when this prophecy was fulfilled in 1967 when, for the first time in nearly 2500 years, since the time Nebuchadnezzar destroyed Jerusalem and took the Jews to Babylon, the Jews had their own city Jerusalem back again.

We know this has to do with *"until the times of the gentiles be fulfilled,"* because Luke 21:27 says, *"and they shall see the Son of man coming"* (Jesus returns to earth). This tells us that the Jews will be dominant at the time of the end, and so will Jerusalem. It seems obvious from all the statements made by Vander Waal, that the Ammillennialist do not believe in the promise of the Lord to Abraham, that the Jews will inherit the land of Canaan forever as God's chosen people.

Therefore, I will go through all the books of the Bible to see what God's word has to say about the Jews inheriting the land of Canaan (Israel) forever, as the Lord has promised to Abraham, Isaac and Jacob again and again.

Genesis 13:15, *"For all the land which thou seest, to thee will I give it, and to thy seed for ever."* How could anyone still say, that the Lord has dismissed Israel after reading the promise God gave to Abraham in this verse?

Genesis 15:13, *"And he said unto Abram; know of a surety that thy seed shall be a stranger in a land that is not theirs, (Egypt) and shall serve them; and they shall afflict them for four hundred years; (the people of Israel were in Egypt 400 years) 14. And also that nation, whom they shall serve, will I judge: and afterwards they shall come out with great substance."*

Did Rev. Verbrugge say that the Bible is not a book foretelling the future? The Lord just did so again here in Genesis 15:13. Because long before it happened, the Lord tells Abraham that the Israelites will be in bondage in Egypt for four hundred years, and that they would leave with very great wealth.

If we would still have doubts that Israel will be the homeland for the Jews forever, read Genesis 15:18, *"In the same day the Lord made a covenant with Abram saying, Unto thy seed have I given this land, from the river of Egypt, unto the great river, the river Euphrates."* Here the Lord Shows how big the future land of Israel will be, from Egypt all the way to the Euphrates River, which is in present day Iraq. This will be the future state of Israel when Jesus comes back to the new earth.

However if we still would not believe that Israel is God's chosen people, read Genesis 48:4, *"... I will make of thee a multitude of people, and will give this land to thy seed after* *thee, for an <u>everlasting</u> possession."* Notice that the Lord says here for an everlasting possession, which means the Lord cannot dismiss the Jews as Vander Waal mentioned.

Genesis 50:24, *"and bring you out of this land unto the land which He sware to Abraham, Isaac, and Jacob."* How could we possibly dismiss this as not being the true word of God?

Exodus 32:13, *"Remember Abraham, Isaac and Israel* (notice the name is now changed) *thy servants, to whom thou swarest by thine own self, and saidst unto them, I will multiply your seed as the stars of heaven, and all this land that I have spoken of, will I give unto your seed, and they shall inherit it for ever."* Here the Lord says again that the Jews will have the land of Israel forever.

Leviticus 26:33, *"And I will scatter you among the heathen ... 42. Then I will remember my covenant with Jacob, and also my covenant with Isaac, and also my covenant with Abraham will I remember; and I will remember the land. 44... neither will I abhor them, to destroy them utterly and to break my covenant with them, for I am the Lord their God."* Here the Lord clearly says that He will not break the covenant He made with Abraham, Isaac, and Jacob.

How can Vander Waal say, "Jesus shows us how the Lord finally dismisses Jerusalem, the city that slaughtered the lamb, Henceforth He will no longer recognize the Jews as His people"?

If we still think that the Lord dismissed the Jews as His people read 1 Chronicles 17:9, *"Also will I ordain a place for my people Israel, and I will plant them, and they shall dwell in their place, and shall be moved no more... 11... I will raise up thy seed after thee, which shall be of thy sons; and I will establish his kingdom. 12. He shall build me an house, and I will establish His throne forever... 14. But I will settle Him in mine house, and in my kingdom for ever: and His throne shall be established for evermore."* It should very clear from this passage of scripture, that the Lord says here He will bring the Jews home again, and they will never leave home again. They will build Him a new temple before Jesus returns to Jerusalem, and His throne will be established there forever more.

2 Chronicles 13:5, *"Ought you not to know that the Lord God of Israel gave the kingdom over Israel to David forever, even to him and to his sons by a covenant of salt?"*

Psalm 89:3, *"I have made a covenant with my chosen, I have sworn unto David my servant, 4. Thy seed will I establish for ever, and build up thy throne to all generations...34. My covenant will I not break, nor alter the thing that is gone out of my lips. 35. Once have I sworn by My Holiness that I will not lie unto David. 36. His seed shall endure forever and his throne as the sun before me."* Here the Lord Himself says that He will not lie about the covenant that He made with David, but that it will be established forever. Is it not amazing how many times the Lord uses the word "forever"? He knew that we would have a problem believing that His covenant with the Jews would be forever.

Psalm 105:8, *"He hath remembered His covenant for ever... 9. Which covenant He made with Abraham; and his oath unto Isaac; 10. And confirmed the same unto Jacob for a law, and to Israel for an everlasting covenant: 11. Saying unto thee will I give the land of Canaan, the lot of your inheritance."* The Lord says here, that He will give the land of Canaan (Israel) to the Jews for ever as an inheritance, as the Lord has promised all through the scriptures.

Jeremiah 23:5, *"Behold, the days come, saith the Lord, that I will raise unto David a righteous Branch (Jesus), and a King shall reign and prosper, and shall execute judgment and justice in the earth."* Here already the Lord foretold the future new earth where Jesus will reign with David. Jeremiah 23:6, *"In his days Judah shall be saved, and Israel shall dwell safely, and this is his name whereby He shall be called,*

THE LORD OUR RIGHTEOUSNESS." Again, it should be clear from this passage that Jeremiah is talking about the future new earth where David will reign with Jesus for ever.

Jeremiah 31:33, *"But this shall be the covenant that I will make with the house of Israel... and* (I) *will be their God, and they shall be my people."*

Jeremiah 46:28, *"Fear thou not, O Jacob my servant, saith the Lord: for I am with thee; for I will make a full end of all the nations whither I have driven thee: but I will not make a full end of thee..."* The Lord says here, that He will punish the nations wherever He has driven the Jews, but that He will not make a full end of Israel. Israel will be forever.

There seems to be no end of verses in the Bible, where the Lord says that Israel is His elect, as in Isaiah 45:4, *"For Jacob my servant's sake, and Israel mine elect, I have even called thee by thy name: I have surnamed thee, though thou hast not known me... 17. But Israel shall be saved in the Lord with an everlasting salvation."*

Chapter 8

"And I will cause the captivity of Judah and the captivity of Israel to return, and will build them, as at the first."
Jeremiah 33:7

—⚊⚊—

We have studied in previous chapters that almost all the books of the Bible proclaim that the Jews are still God's chosen people and they will inherit the land of Israel as their homeland, forever. In this chapter, we will see, that the Lord again says through His prophets, in almost every book of the Bible, that He will bring back the Jews from every nation to their homeland, Israel, to never be uprooted again, but will live there forever.

However the Amillennialist still say, "Dispensationalist teach, that God will establish an earthly kingdom, involving the people of Israel." In his book, Rev. Vander Waal says, "Jesus shows us how the Lord finally dismisses Jerusalem, the city that slaughtered the lamb. Henceforth he will no longer recognize the Jews as His people."

How can he say this, since it was all of us, who through our sins, slaughtered Jesus? It was not just the Jews. As shown in the previous chapters, the Lord forgave the Jews their sin, and they are still God's chosen people, who will inherit the promised land of Israel.

Rev. Hoekema says in CRC Viewpoint, "The teaching that God has a separate purpose for Israel and the church is in error. Dispensationalist often appeal to Romans 11 to support their view on Israel. Remember, that even if we were inclined to understand verses 25-27 as teaching a future national conversion of Israel, we would still have to admit that Romans 11 says nothing whatever about a regathering of Israel to its land or about a future rule of Christ over a millennial Israelite kingdom."

I can not believe that I am reading this, since the Bible shows the opposite, that all through scripture, the prophets talk about "a regathering" of the Jew's to their homeland, as we will see in this chapter.

Jeremiah 30:3, *"For, lo, the days come, saith the Lord, that I will bring again, the captivity of my people Israel and Judah, saith the Lord; and I will cause them to return to their land that I gave to their fathers, and they shall posses it... 9.But they, shall serve the Lord their God, and David their King, whom I shall raise up to them. 10. Therefore fear thou not, O my servant Jacob, saith the Lord; neither be dismayed, O Israel for, lo, I will save thee from afar, and thy seed from the land of their captivity... 22. And ye shall be my people, and I will be your God... 24... in the latter days ye shall consider it."*

Here Jeremiah clearly says that the Jews will return to their homeland, and shall posses it, and they will serve God. It is clear from verse 24, where it says, "In the latter days ye shall consider it," that this points to the time of Jesus return. Also in Jeremiah 23:8, *"But, The Lord liveth, which brought up, and which led the seed of the house of Israel out of the north country, and from all countries whither I had driven them; and they shall dwell in their own land."*

Jeremiah 33:7, *"And I will cause the captivity of Judah and the captivity of Israel to return, and will build them, as at the first."* It is clear from this verse, that not only will the Lord bring them back, but also that the Lord will make them stronger. It should also be clear, that this points again to the latter days, because verse 15 says, *"In those days, and at that time, will I cause the Branch of righteousness to grow up unto David, and He shall execute judgment and righteousness in the land."* This will only happen when Jesus has returned to the new earth, when He reigns with David.

Jeremiah 46:27, *"But fear not thou, O my servant Jacob, and be not dismayed, O Israel: for behold, I will save thee from afar off, and thy seed from the land of their captivity; and Jacob shall return, and be in rest, and at ease, and none shall make him afraid."*

Ezekiel 11:17, *"Therefore say, Thus saith the Lord God: I will even gather you from the people, and assemble you out of the countries where you have been scattered, and I will give you the land of Israel."*

The Lord could not have said it clearer than in this passage of scripture, "And I will give you the land of Canaan." Again it points to the time of the end in verse 20, *"That they may walk in my statutes, and keep mine ordinances, and do them."* Before they were scattered, they did not do His ordinances.

All through the scriptures, in almost all the books of the Bible, the Lord prophesied that the Jew's would come back to their homeland again in the future, and would stay there forever. How can Rev. Hoekema say in CRC Viewpoint, "We would still have to admit, that Romans 11 says nothing whatever about a regathering of Israel to its land, or about a future rule of Christ over a millennium Israelite kingdom."

Even if Romans did not say anything about a "regathering" of the Jews to their homeland, we have to look at all the books of the Bible, where the Lord clearly says that

81

He will "regather" His chosen people the Jews to their own country again.

By the same token, Jesus said that He died for our sins, and we will be saved if we believe in Him, but we don't find this in every book of the Bible either.

Jeremiah 50:20 clearly shows that the Lord will forgive the Jews, *"In those days, and in that time,* (the latter days) *saith the Lord, the iniquity of Israel shall be sought for, and there shall be none; and the sins of Judah, and they shall not be found: for I will pardon them, whom I reserve."* In Micah 7:19 it says, *"and He will subdue our iniquities; and thou wilt cast all their sins into the depths of the sea. 20. Thou wilt perform the truth to Jacob, and the mercy to Abraham, which thou hast sworn unto our fathers from the days of old."* How therefore can the Amillennialist say that the Lord will no longer recognize the Jews as His people?

As we will see in this chapter, already in the first books of the Bible did the Lord prophecy that the Jews would come back again to their homeland forever. Deuteronomy 30:2, *And shalt return to the Lord thy God, and shalt obey His voice according to all that I command thee this day, thou and thy children, with all thine heart, and with all thy soul. 3. That then the Lord thy God, will turn thy captivity, and have compassion upon thee, and will return and gather thee from all the nations whither the Lord thy God hath scattered thee: 5. And the Lord thy God will bring thee into the land which thy fathers possessed, and thou shalt possess it; and he will do thee good, and multiply thee above thy fathers."*

We know that it points to the "latter days" when Jesus returns, because verse 8 says, *"thou shalt return, and obey the voice of the Lord, and do all His commandments which I command thee this day."* They did not do this when Moses wrote this book, but when Jesus returns, they finally will.

In 2 Samuel 7:10 it says, *"Moreover, I will appoint a place for my people Israel, and will plant them, that they may dwell in a place of their own, and move no more; neither shall the children of wickedness afflict them any more, as beforetime."* Again, we know that this is for the "latter days," because verse 13 says, *"He shall build an house* (temple) *for my name, and I will stablish the throne of his kingdom forever."* Since this temple will not be built until the Lord returns, (as in 2 Thess. 2:4) we know that this points to that time. And because it says, "I will establish the throne of His kingdom forever," we know this refers to the end time. Only then will His throne be established forever.

As in 2 Kings 21:7, *"... in this house* (the temple), *and in Jerusalem, which I have chosen out of all tribes of Israel, will I put My name for ever: 8. Neither will I make the feet of Israel move any more out of the land which I gave to their fathers."* Again in 1 Chronicles 17:9, *"Also I will ordain a place for my people Israel, and will plant them, and they shall dwell in their place, and shall be moved no more, neither shall the children of wickedness waste them anymore, as at the beginning... 12. He shall build me an house, and I will stablish his throne for ever... 14. But I will settle him in mine house and in my kingdom for ever: and his throne shall be established for evermore."* This again shows that it is for the "latter day" at the time of Jesus return.

Nehemiah 1:9, *"... yet will I gather them from thence, and will bring them unto the place that I have chosen to set my name there."*

Psalm 14:7, *"Oh, that the salvation of Israel were come out of Zion! when the Lord bringeth back the captivity of His people, Jacob shall rejoice, and Israel shall be glad."*

All through God's word do we see that the Lord will bring the Jews back to their homeland, as in Psalm 85:1-2, *"Lord, thou hast been favourable unto thy land, thou hast brought back the captivity of Jacob. 2. Thou hast forgiven the iniquity of thy people, thou hast covered all their sin,"* Not only does the Lord say in Psalm 85 that the Jews will come back, but also that the Lord has forgiven their sins, contrary to what Vander Waal says in his book on page 139, as we have seen. All through scripture the Lord tells us that the Jews will come back again, as in Isaiah 11:11, *"and it shall come to pass, in that day, that the Lord shall set his hand again the second time* (the first time was to bring the Jews back from Egypt) *to recover the remnant of His people."* This makes it certain, that the Lord is talking here about the future return of His chosen people to Israel.

Isaiah 65:9, *"And I will bring forth a seed out of Jacob, and out of Judah an inheritor of my mountains: and mine elect shall inherit it, and my servants shall dwell there."* The Lord makes it clear here, that His elect (Israel) shall inherit His mountain (Jerusalem) and dwell there. We know that this points to the new earth, because verse 25 says, "The wolf and the lamb shall feed together," which can not happen on this present earth.

Also in Jeremiah 23:3, *"And I will gather the remnant of my flock out of all countries whither I have driven them, and will bring them again to their folds; and they shall be fruitful and increase."* We know that this again points to the new earth, because verse 4 says: *"and they shall fear no more."*

Jeremiah 30:3, *"For, lo, the days come, saith the Lord, that I will bring again the captivity of my people Israel and Judah, saith the Lord: and I will cause them to return to the land that I gave to their fathers, and they shall possess it... 9. But they shall serve the Lord their God, and David their king, whom I will raise up unto them."*

It should be clear from this, that all these prophecies are talking about the "end times" since verse 9 says. *"They shall serve God, and David their king."* which of course, is all in the future. King David had died long before Isaiah wrote this prophecy, and therefore this points to the new earth, when Jesus returns with David.

Jeremiah 30:10, *"Therefore, fear not, O my servant Jacob, saith the Lord; neither be dismayed O Israel: for, lo, I will save thee from afar, and thy seed from the land of captivity; and Jacob shall return, and shall be in rest, and be quiet, and none shall make him afraid."* Jeremiah 31:8, *"Behold, I will bring them from the north country (Russia) and gather them from the coasts of the earth... 10... He that scattered Israel, will gather him, and keep him, as a shepherd doth his flock."*

How can anyone still not believe that the Lord will "regather" His chosen people, as the Amillennialist say?

These passages in scripture repeat over and over again that the Jews will be brought back to their land and will possess it forever, leaving absolutely no doubt that this will happen. Jeremiah, 32:37, *"Behold, I will gather them out of all countries, whither I have driven them in mine anger, and in my fury, and in great wrath; and I will bring them again unto this place, and I will cause them to dwell safely... 40. And I will make an everlasting covenant with them, that I will not turn away from them."*

The Lord says He drove them away in His anger and wrath, yet He will bring them back again. It clearly shows, that the Lord has forgiven the Jews, again contrary to what Vander Waal says in his book. It says He will cause them to dwell safely. This has not yet happened, and reaffirms that this time is yet in the future.

Also in Jeremiah 33:7, *"And I will cause the captivity of Judah, and the captivity of Israel to return, and I will build them, as at the first. 8. And I will cleanse them from all their iniquity ... and I will pardon all their iniquities."* Here again in verse 8 the Lord makes it clear that He will not hold it against them, that the Jews crucified Jesus as Vander Waal says.

All through the Bible does the Lord make it clear, that He is with His chosen people, as in Jeremiah 46:27, *"But thou fear not, O my servant Jacob, and be not dismayed, O*

85

Israel: for behold, I will save thee from afar off, and thy seed from the land of their captivity; and Jacob shall return... 28. Fear thou not, 0 Jacob my servant, saith the Lord: for I am with thee; for I will make a full end of all the nations whither I have driven thee, but I will not make a full end of thee..." Here the Lord makes it clear that He will punish the nations where the Lord had driven His people, but will not make a full end of His people the Jews.

Jeremiah 50:19, *"And I will bring Israel again to his habitation... 20. In those days, and in that time, saith the Lord; the iniquity of Israel shall be sought for, and there shall be none, and the sins of Judah, and they shall not be found: for I will pardon them whom I reserve."* This passage from Jeremiah should make it absolutely certain, that the Jews are still God's chosen people, and He has forgiven them, that they "slaughtered the Lamb."

Amos 9:14, *"And I will bring again the captivity of my people Israel, and they shall build the waste cities, and inhabit them; and they shall plant vineyards, and drink the wine thereof; they also shall make gardens, and eat the fruit of them. 15. And I will plant them upon their land, and they shall no more be pulled up out of their land which I have given them, saith the Lord thy God."* This passage from God's word says it all; His chosen people shall return and make gardens and plant vineyards. It will be their home.

But most of all, they will never again be pulled out of their country, as Amos says here. How are the Amillennialist interpreting this passage of scripture when they say that the Lord has dismissed them as Vander Waal says on page 139 of his book? Or as Rev. Hoekema says in CRC Viewpoint when he comments about Romans 11 saying nothing about a regathering of Israel to its land?

Zephaniah 3:20, *"At that time will I bring you again, even in the time that I gather you: for I will make you a name and a praise among all people of the earth, when I turn back your captivity before your eyes, saith the Lord."* Here the Lord clearly says that the Jews are His chosen people, because the Lord will make them a name and praise among all people of the earth. That must hurt some of us if we still believe that the Lord has dismissed the Jews as His chosen people. Instead, He will assemble them again, as in Micah 2:12, *"I will surely assemble, O Jacob, all of thee; I will surely gather the remnant of Israel; I will put them together..."*

Zechariah 8:7, *"Thus saith the Lord of hosts; Behold, I will save my people from the east country, and from the west country; 8. And I will bring them, and they shall dwell in the midst of Jerusalem: and they shall be my people, and I will be their God, in truth and in righteousness."*

Zechariah 10:6, *"And I will strengthen the house of Judah, and I will save the house of Joseph, and I will bring them again to place them; for I have mercy upon them: and they shall be as though I had not cast them off: for I am the Lord their God, and will hear them."*

Chapter 9

"And thou shalt come up against my people of Israel ... and I will bring thee against my land." Ezekiel 38:16

—ɯ—

Here in Ezekiel 38:16, the Lord calls the land of Israel "my land!" In the book of Joel the Lord also talks about Israel being "my land" as in Joel 3:1-2, *"For, behold, in those days, and in that time, when I shall bring again the captivity of Judah and Jerusalem, 2. I will also gather all nations, and will bring them down into the valley of Jehoshaphat* (the battle of Armageddon) *and will plead with them there for my people and for my heritage Israel, whom they have scattered among the nations, and parted my land."* If the Lord calls the land of Israel "my land", the same land He promised to Abraham, Isaac and Jacob, it would be difficult to believe that the Lord would not bring His chosen people to the land He calls "my land."

Ezekiel 11:16, *"Therefore say, Thus saith the Lord God; Although I have cast them far off among the heathen, and although I have scattered them among the countries, yet will I be to them as a little sanctuary in the countries where they shall come. 17. Therefore say, Thus saith the Lord God; I will even gather you from the people, and assemble you out of the countries where ye have been scattered, and I will give you the land of Israel."* It will be in the "latter days" because verse 20 says, *"That they may walk in my statutes."* Also, in Ezekiel 20:34 it says, *"And I will bring you out from the people, and will gather you out of the countries wherein ye were scattered, with a mighty hand and with a stretched out arm, and with fury poured out. 40. For in mine holy mountain, in the mountain of the height of Israel, saith the Lord God, there shall all the house of Israel, all of them in the land, serve me... 41. I will accept you with your sweet savour, when I bring you out from the people, and gather you out of the countries wherein ye have been scattered; and I will be sanctified in you before the heathen. 42. And ye shall know that I am the Lord, when I shall bring you into the land of Israel, into the country for the which I lifted up mine hand to give it to your fathers."*

Is it not amazing how many times the prophets predict that the Jews will come back to their country? In Ezekiel 28:25, *"Thus saith the Lord God; When I shall have gathered the house of Israel from the people among whom they are scattered, and shall be sanctified in them in the sight of the heathen, then shall they dwell in their land that I have given to my servant Jacob. 26. And they shall dwell safely therein, and shall build houses, and shall plant vineyards; ... and they shall know that I am the Lord their God."*

Ezekiel 34:13, *"And I will bring them out from the people, and gather them from the countries, and will bring them to their own land, and feed them upon the mountains of Israel by the rivers, and in all the inhabited places of the country... 16. I will seek that which was lost, and bring again that which was driven away."* The Lord must have known that we would have problems believing that the Jews would come back home again. Why would He have otherwise instructed the prophets so many times to tell us?

Ezekiel 37:21, *"And say unto them, Thus saith the Lord God; Behold, I will take the children of Israel from among the heathen, whither they be gone, and will gather them on every side, and bring them into their own land. 22. And I will make them one nation in the land upon the mountains of Israel; and one king shall be king to them all: and they shall no more be two nations, neither shall they be divided into two kingdoms any more at all."*

This prophecy was fulfilled on May 14, 1948, when the United Nations officially proclaimed the State of Israel's Independence. There is only one State of Israel, not Israel and Judah, just as Ezekiel prophesied. It is also clear from verse 24 that it points to the new earth, because it says, *"And David my servant shall be king over them; and they all shall have one shepherd: they shall also walk in my judgments, and observe my statutes, and do them."* David will not be King again, until Jesus returns at the beginning of the 1000 year Millennium and then they will observe His statutes.

Ezekiel 37:28, *"And the heathen shall know, that I the Lord do sanctify Israel, when my sanctuary shall be in the midst of them for evermore."*

As we have seen in this chapter as well as in previous chapters, and all through scripture, the Lord prophesied that the Jews would come back home again, and will be blessed for evermore. However in chapter 38 we see that before the Jews will enjoy this prosperous life on the new earth, they will have to go through the 7 year tribulation period, as mentioned by Jesus in Matthew 24:21, *"For then shall be great tribulation such as was not since the beginning of the world to this time, no, nor ever shall be."*

Ezekiel describes clearly this 7 year tribulation period, when the four horsemen from Revelation will go through the world, as we will see in the next chapter. The middle of this 7 year period is when the anti-christ will break his peace covenant as mentioned in Daniel 9:27, *"And in the midst of the week* (seven years) *he* (the anti-christ) *shall cause the sacrifice and the oblation to cease."*

However the Amillennialist do not believe what Ezekiel says here literally, as Vander Waal says in his book on page 19, "Therefore it is foolish to use Ezekiel 38-39 as a source of political predictions about the so-called tribulation period after the rapture ... for what Ezekiel 38 and 39 presents us with in typological fashion is opposition to the gospel."

I will never understand how the Amillennialist can come to this interpretation of Ezekiel, but then, if you interpreted the tribulation with, "a source of political predictions about the so-called tribulation," that does not speak highly of Jesus' passage from Matthew 24:21. I find it curious that anyone who believes the Bible to be the word of God could even suggest that one part of the Bible opposes another.

As we will see in this chapter, Ezekiel's prophecy looks more like a prophecy directly from the Lord, given by His prophet, than writings in "typological fashion" that are in "opposition to the gospel," as Vander Waal calls it.

In Ezekiel 38 we find a list of nations that form a huge army and go to attack the land of Israel. Ezekiel 38:8 says, *"After many days thou shalt be visited: in the latter years, thou shalt come into the land that is brought back from the sword, and is gathered out of many people, against the mountains of Israel, which have been always waste: but it is brought forth out of the nations, and they shall dwell safely all of them. 9. Thou shalt ascend and come like a storm... 11. And thou shalt say, I will go up to the land of unwalled villages; I will go to them that are at rest, that dwell safely... 12. To take a spoil, and to take a prey."* This prophecy from Ezekiel seems to me fairly easy to understand. The passage "in the latter years" points to the end time just before Jesus returns and it is clear that "the land" mentioned is Israel, and the people are living safely in "unwalled villages." The reason for this peaceful existence is because the anti-christ has made a 7 year peace treaty as prophesied in Daniel 9:27, *"and he* (the anti-christ) *shall confirm the covenant with many* (many nations) *for one week* (seven years)." The reason for the attack is spelled out in Ezekiel 38:12, *"To take a spoil, and to take a prey: to turn thine hand upon the desolate places that are now inhabited, and upon the people that are gathered out of the nations, which have gotten cattle and goods, that dwell in the midst of the land."*

It is clear that verse 12 points to the Jews that have just come back to the promised land of Israel, since it says, *"the people that are gathered out of the nations."* In verse 14 it says, *"Therefore, son of man, prophesy and say unto Gog, Thus saith the Lord God; In that day when my people of Israel dwelleth safely, shalt thou not know it? 15. And thou shalt come from thy place out of the north parts, thou, and many people with thee ... a mighty army. 16. And thou shalt come up against my people Israel, as a cloud to cover the land; it shall be in the latter days, and I will bring thee against my land, that the heathen may know me, when I shall be sanctified in thee, O Gog, before their eyes."*

Ezekiel says, "From thy place out of the north parts," and tells us in verse 2 that Gog will come from the land of "Magog" a nation of three parts; Rosh, Meshech, and Tubal. Genesis 10:1-2 says, *"Now these are the generations of the sons of Noah, Shem, Ham, and Japheth: and unto them were sons born after the flood. 2. The sons of Japheth; Gomer, and Magog, and Madai, and Javan, and Tubal, and Meshech, and Tiras."*

Ezekiel 38:1-6, *"And the word of the Lord came unto me, saying, 2. Son of man, set thy face against gog, the land of Magog, the chief prince of Meshech and Tubal, and prophesy against him, 3. And say, Thus saith the Lord God; Behold, I am against thee, O Gog, the chief prince of Meshech and Tubal: 4. And I will turn thee back, and put hooks into thy jaws, and I will bring thee forth and all thine army... 5. Persia, Ethiopia, and Libya with them; all of them with shield and helmet: 6. Gomer, and all his bands; the house of Togarmah of the north quarters and all his bands."*

The Amillennialist do not take Ezekiel literally, as Vander Waal says on page 78, "Goggology, Russia – Gog, that's another of Hal Lindsay's axioms ... it all falls neatly into place in Lindsay's 'Goggology'." However, instead of making fun of Ezekiel's prophecies, we would do well to take it seriously, as written in 2 Peter 1:19, *"We have also a more sure word of prophecy; whereunto ye do well that ye take heed."* Take it seriously because there is a reason that God told his prophets to write about this "north place." There are other references to it as well. Jeremiah 16:14, *"Therefore, behold, the days come saith the Lord, that it shall no more be said, The Lord liveth, that brought the children of Israel out of the land of Egypt; 15. But, The Lord liveth, that brought up the children of Israel from the land of the north, and from all the lands whither He had driven them."*

This prophecy was fulfilled, when Russia temporarily opened its borders, so that even the Jews from the USSR could go back to Israel, which had not been possible under communist rule. Jeremiah mentions this again in Jeremiah 23:7-8, and also in 31:8, *"Behold, I will bring them from the north country..."*

Jeremiah 1:14, *"Then the Lord said unto me, Out of the north an evil shall break forth upon all the inhabitants of the land."* Is this not an amazing passage of scripture? It says exactly the same thing as Ezekiel 38:8, and therefore we certainly can take Ezekiel's prophecy literally.

Jeremiah 1:13, *"And the word of the Lord came unto me the second time, saying, What seest thou? And I said, I see a seething pot and the face thereof is towards the north."*

Also in Joel 2:20, *"But I will remove far off from you the northern army and will drive him into a land barren and desolate, with his face towards the east sea, and his hinder part towards the utmost sea."* Here the Lord says that this northern army, which is invading Israel, will be pushed back to Siberia, as Ezekiel describes it.

Since this "northern place" is mentioned so often in the scriptures, we can certainly take Ezekiel's prophecies literally. And since Ezekiel says in verse 8, *"In the latter years thou salt be visited,"* we know this will happen in the end times and this points to the time of Jesus' return to the new earth. Even more so, when we read Ezekiel 38:17, *"Thus saith the Lord God, Art thou he of whom I have spoken in old time by my servants the prophets of Israel, which prophesied in those days many years, that I would bring thee against them?"*

This an amazing passage from the Bible, where the Lord Himself says that He has spoken in old times, through the prophets, that this would happen. God Himself makes a point of tying these prophesies together to tell the doubtful to take it literally. It will happen!

Ezekiel 38:18, *"And it shall come to pass at the same time when Gog shall come against the land of Israel, saith the Lord God; that my fury shall come up in my face."*

Ezekiel 39:1 *"Therefore, thou son of man, prophecy against Gog and say, Thus saith the Lord God; Behold, I am against thee O Gog, the chief prince of Meshech and Tubal: 2. And I will turn thee back, and leave but the sixth part of thee, and will cause thee to come up from the north parts, and will bring thee upon the mountains of Israel."* Ezekiel 39 confirms here what Ezekiel 38 already said, that the people from the north (Russia) will come against the mountains of Israel. Notice how God is repeating Himself here to impress upon us how serious He is. How can anyone still not believe, and not take this literally as the true word of God?

In Ezekiel 39:4 it says, *"Thou shalt fall upon the mountains of Israel, thou, and all thy bands, and all the people that is with thee."* Even though the armies that come to attack Israel will be overwhelming, they will be defeated. God Himself promises He will intervene and defend His chosen people, the Jews. He will destroy them. Here the Lord again fulfills His promise that He would bring the Jews back home again, for the enemy armies will not prevail over Israel, but Israel will continue to live in their homeland.

The Lord says in verse 6, *"And I will send a fire on Magog, and among them that dwell carelessly in the isles: that they may know that I am the Lord. 7. So will I make my Holy name known in the midst of my people Israel; and I will not let them pollute my Holy name any more: and the heathen shall know, that I am the Lord, the Holy One in Israel."* This makes it clear why the enemy will not prevail, because the Lord has stated that He will take care of His chosen people Israel for the entire world to see. As the Lord said, *"The heathen shall know that I am the Lord."* Ezekiel 39:8, *"Behold, it is come, and it is done, saith the Lord God; this is the day whereof I have spoken."* Again, the Lord says that He has foretold this through the prophets; and that this prophecy will be fulfilled as a literal event for the entire world to see and understand.

It is hard to believe therefore, that the Amillennialist will not take this literally, but instead interpret this as symbolic. To take all this as symbolic is hard to understand, especially when we read Ezekiel 39:21, *"And I will set my glory among the heathen and all the heathen shall see my judgments that I have executed, and my hand that I have laid upon them, 22. So the house of Israel shall know, that I am the Lord their God from that day forward. 23. And the heathen shall know that the house of Israel went into captivity for their iniquity: because they trespassed against me, therefore hid I my face from them, and gave them into the hand of their enemies: so fell they all by the sword."* This is an amazing passage from scripture again, as we see that the Lord has forgiven the Jews also, after the Lord had punished them. This in direct contrast to what Vander Waal said; "Jesus shows us how the Lord finally dismisses Jerusalem, the city that slaughtered the Lamb. Henceforth He will no longer recognize the Jews as His people."

I sincerely hope, that by now, through all that the prophets have shown us in their prophecies, that we can believe what the Lord says here. That He has indeed forgiven the Jews. This is also very clear in Ezekiel 39:25-29, where the Lord says, *"Therefore thus said the Lord God; Now will I bring again the captivity of Jacob* (since The Lord Himself changed the name of Jacob to Israel, we can read, Israel), *and have mercy upon the whole house of Israel, and will be jealous for my holy name; 26. After that they have borne their shame and all their trespasses whereby they have trespassed against me, when they dwelt safely in their land, and none made them afraid. 27. When I have brought them again from the people, and gathered them out of their enemies' lands, and am sanctified in them in the sight of many nations: 28. Then shall they know that I am the Lord their God, which caused them to be led into captivity among the heathen: but I have gathered them unto their own land, and have left none of them any more there. 29. Neither will I hide my face any more from them: for I have poured out my spirit upon the house of Israel, saith the Lord God."*

This is a remarkable passage from scripture, where the Lord clearly says that after He has regathered the Jews to their own land, He is sanctified in them, and will bless them, and will never hide His face any more from them. Anyone who still believes that the Lord has dismissed the Jews, should read this over again.

Ezekiel chapter 40 deals with the future temple still to be built, as do chapters 41, 42, and 43. Ezekiel 44 is a remarkable chapter that deals with the East gate in Jerusalem, which will be shut, until Jesus returns to the Mount of Olives, and will go through the East gate again to enter Jerusalem. Ezekiel 44:1 says, *"Then He brought me back the way of the gate of the outward sanctuary which looketh toward the east, and it was shut. 2. Then said the Lord unto me; This gate shall be shut, it shall not be opened, and no man shall enter by it, because the Lord, the God of Israel, hath entered in by it, therefore it shall be shut."* Ezekiel is saying here, that the Eastern gate will be shut, because Jesus entered Jerusalem through it on Palm Sunday before He was crucified. The Lord says it will be shut until Jesus returns to the Mount of Olives when He will enter through it again. Ezekiel 44:3, *"It is for the prince (Jesus): the prince, He shall sit in it to eat bread before the Lord; He shall enter by the way of the porch of that gate, and shall go out by the way of the same."* It is clear from Ezekiel 47 that much of this book deals with the end times, as in Ezekiel 47:12, *"And by the river upon the bank thereof, on this side and on that side, shall grow all trees for meat, whose leaf shall not fade, neither shall the fruit thereof be consumed: it shall bring forth new fruit according to his months, because their waters they issued out of the sanctuary: and the fruit thereof shall be for meat, and the leaf thereof for medicine."*

Here the Lord says that there will be plenty of food in the new earth, and that the leaves will be used for medicine. Anyone who still interprets Ezekiel as symbolic, will have a problem with this passage, because the Lord clearly says that it will be so. Ezekiel 47:13 deals with outlining the borders of the future kingdom of Israel, as in Ezekiel 47:13, *"Thus saith the Lord God; This shall be the border, whereby ye shall inherit the land according to the twelve tribes of Israel..."* And then it describes the border for each tribe of Israel. Ezekiel 47:22, *"And it shall come to pass, that ye shall divide it by lot for an inheritance unto you, and to the strangers that sojourn among you, which shall beget children among you: And they shall be unto you as born in the country among the children of Israel; they shall have inheritance with you among the tribes of Israel. 23. And it shall come to pass, that in what tribe the stranger sojourneth, there shall you give him his inheritance, saith the Lord God."*

This is also an amazing passage from scripture, where the Lord says that the sojourner, not being an Israelite, will also have the same inheritance as people of Israel. It still is clear however, that the people of Israel are God's chosen people, whether we like to believe this or not. This also reinforces the fact that God is speaking specifically about the Jews and not symbolically about the church. God's word keeps mentioning this all the time, so that we cannot be mistaken about it.

Ezekiel 48:19, *"And they that serve the city shall serve it out of all the tribes of Israel... 35... and the name of the city from that day shall be, The Lord is Here."*

Chapter 10

The Four Horsemen *"...behold a white horse ... and he went forth conquering, and to conquer."* **Rev. 6:2**

—⚓︎—

Revelation 6:1, *"And I saw when the Lamb opened one of the seals, and I heard as it were, the noise of thunder..."* The opening of this first seal ushers in the tribulation, a 7 year period that begins with the anti-christ signing a seven year covenant with Israel, shortly after the Rapture. This tribulation concludes with the glorious return of Jesus at the end of the battle of Armageddon, as we will see in the next chapter. From the end of the battle of Armageddon, until Jesus Christ destroys the anti-christ, will be the "great" day of God's wrath. Revelation 6:17, *"For the great day of His wrath is come, and who shall be able to stand?"*

According to Revelation chapter 6, this will be a terrible time on earth. This is the time when the seals of judgment are opened and the four horsemen will begin their ride on earth to bring the wrath of God. The seals are the seven seals of the book of life, which only Jesus can open, and He does this at the time of the end, after he has raptured His church. (Read Revelation chapter 5.)

Revelation 6:2, *"And I saw, and behold a <u>white</u> horse: and he that sat on him had a bow ... and he went forth* *conquering, and to conquer... 3. And when He had opened the second seal... 4... there went out another horse that was* <u>red</u>*: and power was given to him that sat thereon to take peace from the earth, that they should kill one another: ... 5. And when He had opened the third seal ... a* <u>black</u> *horse; and he that sat on him had a pair of balances in his hand... 7. And when He had opened the fourth seal ... 8. And I looked, and behold a* <u>pale</u> *horse: and his name that sat on him was Death, and Hell followed with him."*

However the Amillennialist do not believe that things will be any worse than they are now, as Rev Verbrugge says in his sermons about Revelation. He says, "We are not waiting for the four horsemen. They are here already, have been here since John wrote Revelation. They ride in our world now." Why is it that Amillennialist do not believe that there will be a terrible tribulation time such as we have never seen before? That this will happen just before Jesus returns, as Jesus Himself says in Matthew 24:21, *"For 'then'* (at the time of the end) *shall be 'great' tribulation such as was not since the beginning of the world to this time, no, nor ever shall be,"* How can one interpret what Jesus says here, to mean that there have always been terrible tribulations, and that there have always been four horsemen riding on earth, as Verbrugge says? Jesus clearly says, "then shall be great tribulation such as was not since the beginning of the world, no, nor ever shall be."

From this passage we see that there will be only one terrible time when the four horsemen are riding on earth and that will be just before Jesus returns. Jesus Himself says in Matthew 24:29, *"Immediately after the tribulation of those days* (the days that the four horsemen are riding), *shall the sun be darkened, and the moon shall not give her light, and the stars shall fall from heaven, and the powers of the heavens shall be shaken: 30. And then shall appear the sign of the Son of man in heaven: and then shall all the tribes of the earth mourn, and they shall see the Son of man coming in the clouds of heaven, with power and great glory."* If one would still be in doubt as to whether or not the four horsemen have always been riding on earth, instead of only at the time of the end, this passage from scripture should make it clear. Matthew 24:29 clearly says that after this great tribulation the sun shall be darkened, and the moon shall not give her light. We all know that this has not happened yet, and therefore this "great" tribulation is yet to come. There are many places in scripture where the Lord refers to the darkening of the sun and the moon. Isaiah 13:10, *"For the stars of heaven and the constellations thereof shall not give their light: the sun shall be darkened in his going forth, and the moon shall not cause her light to shine."*

If one would say that this has nothing to do with the end time, they should read Isaiah 13:9, the previous verse, *"Behold, the day of the Lord cometh, cruel both with wrath and fierce anger, to lay the land desolate: and he shall destroy the sinners thereof out of it."* Here again, it points to the end time, the same as in Matthew 24:29. Also in Joel 2:10, *"The earth shall quake before them; the heavens shall tremble: the sun and the moon shall be dark, and the stars shall withdraw their shining."* And as if this would not be clear enough yet, Revelation 6:12 says, *"And I beheld when He had opened the sixth seal, and, lo, there was a great earthquake; and the sun became black as sackcloth of hair, and the moon became blood."*

Revelation 8:12, *"And the fourth angel sounded, and the third part of the sun was smitten, and the third part of the moon, and the third part of the stars; so as the third part of them was darkened, and the day shone not for a third part of it, and the night likewise."* However, the Amillennialist still do not believe that all these horrendous things, like the four horsemen riding, are just for the end times. Rev Verbrugge says in his sermons about Revelation, "We are not waiting for the four horsemen, they are here already. Have been here since John wrote Revelation. They ride in our world now." If this would be so, why then does Revelation say that those terrible events will happen at the time of the end, when Jesus is about to return, as is written in Rev. 6:12, *"And I beheld when He had opened the sixth seal, and, lo, there was a great earthquake: and the sun became black as sackcloth of hair, and the moon became as blood."*

After reading this passage, how could anyone say that this happens all the time; that these horsemen have been riding on the earth always. It is clear from Rev. 6:12, that they will not ride till the sun becomes dark and the moon as blood, which of course has not happened yet. Also, in verse 13, *"And the stars of heaven fell even as a fig tree casteth her untimely figs, when she is shaken of a mighty wind. 14... and every mountain and island were moved out of their places. 15. And the kings of the earth, and the great men, and the rich men, and the chief captains, and the mighty men, and every bond man, and every free man, hid themselves in the dens and in the rocks of the mountains."* This passage shows clearly how bad it will be when the four horseman start to ride on earth.

Verse 16, *"And said to the mountains, and to the rocks, Fall on us, and hide us from the face of Him that sitteth on the throne, and from the wrath of the Lamb: 17. For the great day of His wrath is come, and who shall be able to stand?"* This passage shows again how horrendous the wrath of God will be, and asks, "who will be able to stand?" It is a comfort therefore to believe that we will be raptured before all of this, if we are His children. Revelation 9:18 also shows how bad it will be. *"By these three was the third part of men killed, by the fire and by the smoke, and by the brimstone which issued out of their mouths."*

Rev. Verbrugge says, "These bizarre events are relative to our time. However the plagues of the four horsemen will

104

not harm the people of God. One third of every plague means it is limited." If one calls one third of all men killed "limited" then why can we simply not believe what Revelation says? Rev. 9:12, *"One woe is past; and, behold, there come two woes more hereafter."* When things are so bad, that the people want the mountains to fall on them, I do not interpret this as "limited."

Through all these passages from scripture, it seems very clear that they are meant to be taken literally, knowing that terrible times will come at the end times as Jesus said they will. Rev. Vander Waal however has a different opinion of the 'end time' as mentioned on page 83 of his book. "Misconceptions about Bible prophecy lead to misunderstanding in the area of exegesis. When Daniel talks about the 'time of the end' (vs. 4 and 9) some translations and interpretations turn this into the 'end time'. This in turn fosters the notion that Daniel's visions deal with the absolute end of history. The expression 'the last days' which is used by some of the other prophets, has furthered the same misunderstanding."

It should be clear from this that Vander Waal thinks that the words "end times" and "the last days" used by the prophets is a misunderstanding. He refuses to take God's word literally, when God says "end time" or "the last days." He refuses to believe that it indeed points to what it says – "the last days"? Why do Amillennialist believe that nothing will change until Jesus returns? No rapture, no worse tribulation than what we have always had, same four horsemen riding as they have always been riding on earth, no anti-christ, no Armageddon, no Millennium, etc.? Everything will just stay the same, as it always was, with no real problems, as mentioned previously. They assume everything will just continue as it always has until Jesus returns: month from now, or perhaps 1000 years from today, or maybe even today.

This is why the apostle Peter says in 2 Peter 3:1, *"This second epistle beloved, I now write unto you, in both which*

I stir up your pure minds by way of remembrance: 2. That ye may be mindful of the words which were spoken before by the holy prophets, and of the commandments of us the apostles of the Lord and Savior: 3. Knowing this first, that there shall come in the last days ... scoffers... 4 ... saying, Where is the promise of His coming? For since the fathers fell asleep, all things continue as they were from the beginning of the creation. 5. For this they willingly are ignorant of, that by the word of God the heavens were of old, and the earth standing out of the water, and in the water: 6. Whereby the world that then was, being overflowed with water, perished: 7. But the heavens and the earth, which are now, by the same word are kept in store, reserved unto fire against the day of judgment and perdition of ungodly men. 8. But, beloved, be not ignorant of this one thing, that one day is with the Lord as a thousand years, and a thousand years as one day... 10. But the day of the Lord will come as a thief in the night... and the elements will melt away with fervent heat."

Here the apostle Peter does not take it lightly, that we would believe that everything will continue as it has always been. Verse 10 says; "the elements will melt with fervent heat," - an exact description of an atomic blast, as also mentioned in Joel 2:30, *"And I will show wonders in the heavens and in the earth, blood, and fire, and pillars of smoke."* Again, a description of atomic warfare, which Ezekiel also mentions in Ezekiel 38:22, *"And I will plead against him with pestilence and with blood: and I will rain upon him, and upon his bands, and upon the many people are with him, an overflowing rain, and great hailstones, fire, and brimstone."*

Also in Revelation 9:18, *"By these three was the third part of men killed, by the fire, and by the smoke, and by the brimstone, which issued out of their mouths."*

How could anyone not take this literally, and not believe what the Lord says here in these different passages from the

Bible? This is what it will be like during the tribulation period after the four horsemen start riding on the earth, and God's final series of judgments upon the earth, as in Revelation 8:7, *"and the third part of trees was burnt up, and all the green grass was burnt up,"* This could easily be the result of atomic warfare as discussed earlier. Verse 9 says, *"And the third part of the creatures which were in the seas, and had life, died; and the third part of the ships were destroyed. 10. And the third angel sounded, and there fell a great star from heaven, burning as it were a lamp, and it fell upon the third part of the rivers, and upon the fountains of waters;"* Luke 21:25 says, *"And there shall be signs in the sun, and in the moon, and in the stars; ... the sea and the waves roaring."* This could well be another tidal wave, or "tsunami" as we have seen recently, however, on an even much bigger scale. Verse 13 of Revelation 8 says, *"...Woe, woe, woe, to the inhabiters of the earth by reason of the other voices of the trumpet of the three angels, which have yet to sound!"*

Not only in Revelation, but all through the Bible, have the prophets prophesied that terrible things would happen in "the last days" when the four horseman start riding on earth, and the seven seals of judgment are opened. In Isaiah 13:11, God says, *"And I will punish the world for their evil, and the wicked for their iniquity; and will cause the arrogancy of the proud to cease... 13. Therefore I will shake the heavens and the earth shall remove out of her place, in the wrath of the Lord of hosts, and in the day of His fierce anger."*

Isaiah 26:21, *"For, behold, the Lord cometh out of His place to punish the inhabitants of the earth for their iniquity:"*

Jeremiah 25:29, *"For, lo, I begin to bring evil on the city which is called by My name, and should ye be utterly unpunished? Ye shall not be unpunished: for I will call for a sword upon all the inhabitants of the earth, saith the Lord of hosts. 30. Therefore prophesy thou against them all these words, and say unto them, The Lord shall roar from on high... 31... He will plead with all flesh; He will give them that are wicked to the sword, saith the Lord... 33. And the slain of the Lord shall be at that day from one end of the earth, even unto the other end of the earth:"*

Haggai 2:6, *"For thus saith the Lord of hosts; Yet once, it is a little while and I will shake the heavens, and the earth, and the sea, and the dry land."*

It is clear that this points to the end time, because verse 7 says, *"And I will shake all nations, and the desire of all nations shall come, and I will fill this house* (the future new temple) *with glory, saith the Lord of hosts... 9. The glory of this latter house* (the new temple yet to be built) *shall be greater than of the former* (the old Herodian temple), *saith the Lord of hosts: and in this place* (the new temple) *will I give peace, saith the Lord of hosts."* This is a very powerful passage of scripture, where the Lord Himself says that the glory of this new temple to be built yet, will be much greater then the old temple, and that He will give peace from the new temple. After reading this, how could anyone still not believe that there will be a future temple?

Zephaniah 1:2, *"I will utterly consume all things from the land, saith the Lord. 3. I will consume man and beast... and I will cut off man from the land, saith the Lord... 14. The great day of the Lord is near, it is near... 15. That day is a day of wrath, a day of trouble and distress, a day of waste- ness and desolation, a day of darkness and gloominess, a day of clouds and thick darkness... 17. And I will bring distress upon men, and they shall walk like blind men... 18. Neither their silver nor their gold shall be able to deliver them in the day of the Lord's wrath: but the whole land shall be devoured by the fire of His jealousy: for He shall make even a speedy riddance of all them that dwell in the land,"*

This passage shows how great the wrath of the Lord will be during the tribulation time. Also in Zechariah 12:4

it says, *"In that day, saith the Lord, I will smite every horse with astonishment, and his rider with madness..."* Again and again the Lord shows how bad it will be when the four horsemen start riding on earth. Of course, if, as an Amillennialist I would not believe in the Rapture, or the 7 year tribulation, or Armageddon, or the anti-christ ruling the world during this time of unspeakable horror, then I would simply pray that the Lord would keep me safe through this difficult time. However, the Lord says in Revelation 3:10, *"I also will keep thee from the hour of temptation, which shall come upon all the world, to try them that dwell upon the earth."* Here the Lord clearly says, that He will keep His believers from going through this hour (the 7 year tribulation) which shall come upon all the world. Notice that the Lord says here, "upon all the world."

We therefore can not say that Rev. 3:10 points to tribulations that have occurred all through the ages, but clearly to the final 7 year tribulation period. Jesus says in Matthew 24:32, *"Now learn a parable of the fig tree; When his branch is yet tender, and putteth forth leaves, ye know that summer is nigh: 33. So likewise ye, when ye shall see all these things, know that it is near, even at the doors."* Similarly, Mark 13:28-29, says that we will recognize the signs. Also in Luke 21:30-31, Jesus says that we will know when His coming is near.

Luke 21:24 says, *"And they shall fall by the edge of the sword, and shall be led away captive into all nations: and Jerusalem shall be trodden down of the Gentiles, until the times of the Gentiles be fulfilled."* This is listed as one of the signs by which we could know that Jesus' return is near. We've seen from previous chapters, that this prophecy was fulfilled in June 1967, when, for the first time since Nebuchadnezzar took the Jews to Babylon almost 2500 years ago, Jerusalem was again in the hands of Israel. Just as Luke 21:21 had prophesied, that the Jews would be led away captive, till the times of the Gentiles be fulfilled, most of Israel became a country again on May 14, 1948, except for Jerusalem, which happened in June of 1967. Jesus is telling us that after the "time of the gentiles" Jerusalem will no longer be trodden down, and this also tells us it will belong to the Jews since the "gentiles" will no longer be a factor.

There are of course many other signs that the coming of Jesus is near, even at the door. For instance, we can look at the terrible violence on earth right now, which was also foretold by the word of God. Jesus says in Luke 17:26, *"And as it was in the days of Noah, so shall it be also in the days of the Son of man. 27. They did eat, they drank, they married wives, they were given in marriage, until the day that Noah entered into the ark, and the flood came, and destroyed them all. 28. Likewise also as it was in the days of Lot: they did eat, they drank, they bought, they sold, they planted, they builded: 29. But the same day that Lot went out of Sodom it rained fire and brimstone from heaven, and destroyed them all. 30. Even thus shall it be in the day when the Son of man is revealed."* It is not difficult to understand what Luke is saying here, that when the violence on earth is as bad as in Noah's days, we will know that the return of Jesus is near, even at the door. We can also see the parallel here in that God removed Noah and Lot and their families before sending his punishment. So too will the church be removed in the rapture, before God sends his final judgments upon the earth.

It is also not difficult to see that the violence today is as bad as in Noah's days, as we read in Genesis 6:11, *"The earth was corrupt before God, and the earth was filled with violence. 12. And God looked upon the earth, and, behold, it was corrupt; for all flesh had corrupted his way upon the earth. 13. And God said unto Noah, The end of all flesh is come before Me; for the earth is filled with violence through them: and, behold, I will destroy them with the earth."* One might say that the violence today is not nearly as bad as in Noah's days. However, even Rev. Verbrugge said, "The four horsemen represent broken family life. There are more divorces than ever before. There is more violence in the streets and in the Middle East. Everything is falling apart in the world with violent culture of death, from the terrible calamities of the four horsemen." I most certainly agree with Rev. Verbrugge here, although I was a little surprised after he said previously that we do not have to wait for the four horsemen, that they are here already and have been here, since John wrote Revelation.

It should be obvious however, from all the passages of scripture that I have previously discussed, that the four horsemen will not be riding on earth, until the tribulation period begins. But the violence in the world has already reached frightening proportions, and will increase as we come closer to the return of Jesus. Luke 21:9, *"But when you shall hear of wars and commotions, be ye not terrified: for these things must first come to pass; but the end is not by and by."*

We can certainly see the increase of violence in the world today. Like "home invasions," which we had never heard of before, but lately, this violence is mentioned almost daily in the news. Home invasions often end in injury or even death from the violent break-ins. Also, "suicide bombers" are in the news a lot these days. This is a term that was new to our society, but has now become commonplace. These violent events are happening far too often, and in many different places lately, not only in the middle east any more.

Then we also have the "terrorist attacks" of late. Again, this is a term of the present time, indicating violence that is relatively new to us. Not just on 9-11 in New York, but also in London, Madrid, Moscow, Bali, Egypt, and this list continues to grow. All these things make it clear that the four horsemen are about to begin their fearsome rides on earth. Jesus tells us how bad it will get in Matthew 24:6, *"And you shall hear of wars and rumors of war; see that ye be not troubled: for all these things must come to pass, but the end is not yet. 7. For nation shall rise against nation, and kingdom against kingdom:* (pointing to all the civil wars we have at the present time) *and there shall be famines,* (we have had many, and there is presently a terrible famine in Africa, which could cause hundreds of thousands of deaths) *and earthquakes, in divers places."* Scientists tell us that we have had more earthquakes in the last 10 years than in the previous 100 years. Matthew 24:8, *"All these are the beginning of sorrows"*

Jesus is pointing out here in Matthew 24, that despite the troubles and problems of the world, things will get worse just before the end, i.e. when the four horsemen start riding. One might ask how we know that these problems point to the return of Jesus? Because Jesus says in Matthew 24:29, *"Immediately after the tribulation* (the terrible things mentioned previously in Matthew 24), *shall the sun be darkened, and the moon shall not give her light, and the stars shall fall from heaven, and the powers of the heavens shall be shaken: 30. And then shall appear the sign of the Son of man in the heaven..."* Matthew makes it clear that the troubles and wickedness of the world will increase exponentially toward the time of the end. They will NOT simply carry on as always. And Jesus tells us that this will be our indication that He will be returning soon. The four horsemen will only be riding just before Jesus returns during the tribulation period. Matthew 24:21 says, *"For then shall be great tribulation such as was not since the beginning of the world..."* This eliminates the possibilities that there have always been tribulations in the world, as bad as the great tribulation of Matthew 24:21.

Another indicator of His imminent return is the change in weather patterns. The weather is changing due to global warming. We have more category 5 hurricanes, and more violent tornadoes, than ever before. More frequent floods and violent storms everywhere, as Jesus said in Luke 21:25,

"And there shall be signs in the sun, and the moon, and the stars; and upon the earth distress of nations with perplexity: the sea and the waves roaring." Again Jesus makes it clear that these things will not happen until He is about to return, because verse 27 says, *"And then shall they see the Son of man coming in a cloud with power and great glory."* Again and again the scriptures tell us that these terrible events will happen in the latter days, just before His return.

There will also be more diseases than ever before, like Aids and the bird flu, which is new in the past few yeas, and as the World Health Organization says, could lead to a flu pandemic where literally hundreds of thousands could die. Other diseases, which have been dormant for many years, have come back again, like TB and the mumps. That this would happen before the end times has all been prophesied in scripture. Jesus says this in Matthew 24:7, *"...and there shall be famines, and pestilences, and earthquakes, in divers places."*

As I am writing about the terrible things that will happen when the four horsemen start riding in the world, right this very day, children in Canada and the United States are rallying to be heard, to stop the genocide that is happening today at Darfur in the Sudan, where hundreds of thousands are about to die from starvation, unless the western world comes to their rescue. Will the western world be in time to avoid this genocide? Or will it be too late? Are we that close to the four horsemen to begin their ride on earth? Could the rapture happen at any time, so that Christ's believers will not have to go through the great tribulation, as Jesus says in Matthew 24? I am sure that His believers in Darfur will be praying that He is coming for His church and that the rapture will be soon.

There are so many more things that Jesus prophesied would happen before He returns. His name will be blasphemed as it says in Revelation 13:6, *"And he opened his mouth in blasphemy against God, to blaspheme His name, and His tabernacle, and them that dwell in heaven."* Also, in Revelation 16:9, *"And men were scorched with great heat, and blasphemed the name of God, which had power over these plagues: and they repented not to give Him glory."* It is mentioned in many more places in the Bible that His name will be blasphemed in the "latter days."

These passages point to the rapture being close, and the start of the seven year tribulation after the rapture. The Lord's name is blasphemed today in the movies and on television, as well as almost everywhere else, like never before. A very real sign that His coming is near, is the "Da Vinci Code," first the book, and now the movie, where the Lord Jesus Christ is blasphemed against in the most horrendous way, as having had sex with Mary Magdalene, and produced a child. What a terrible, blaspheming book and movie.

I am admiring Jack Van Impe for taking a firm stand against this and speaking out against this movie in many of his programs lately. He really tries hard to tell the world to protest against this horrendous movie, and to boycott it as much as possible. We will continue to pray, that the Lord will give him the strength to fight against the evil that this movie obviously is.

Chapter 11

"...and saw a beast rise up out of the sea..." Revelation 13:1

—〰—

Revelation 13:1, *"And I stood upon the sand of the sea, and saw a beast* (the anti-christ) *rise up out of the sea, having seven heads and ten horns, and upon his horns ten crowns, and upon his heads the name of blasphemy."* Rev. 13:1 says "having seven heads and ten horns." The seven heads point to the seven empires from king Nebuchadnezzar's dream as we have seen in previous chapters. Egypt and Assyria had already fallen, when Nebuchadnezzar came to power in Babylon, which was then taken by the Medo-Persians, who were later conquered by Greece. Greece is the third empire from Nebuchadnezzar's dream, as mentioned in Daniel 7:23, and is actually the fifth empire, since Egypt and Assyria had already fallen before Babylon came to power. That was when Daniel wrote about king Nebuchadnezzar's dream in the book of Daniel. Greece was taken by Rome, as we have seen in previous chapters, so Rome became the sixth empire described in Daniel. Daniel 2:40, *"And the fourth kingdom shall be strong as iron: forasmuch as iron breaketh in pieces and subdueth all things: and as iron that breaketh all these, shall it break in pieces and bruise. 41. And whereas thou sawest the feet and toes, part of potter's clay, and part of iron, the kingdom shall be divided; but there shall be in it of the strength of the iron, forasmuch as thou sawest the iron mixed with miry clay. 42. And as the toes of the feet were part iron, and part of clay, so the kingdom shall be partly strong, and partly broken.*" Is it not amazing how the Lord, through Daniel, foretold what would happen in the future? That this fourth kingdom in Nebuchadnezzar's dream (the Roman Empire) would not totally be conquered by other nations, and disappear completely, but instead, would come back at the time of the end, as the European Union of today.

The European Union started in 1948 as the Benelux, then grew to 10 nations, as we have seen in previous chapters, and is presently already 23 nations strong. It will be reinstated as the 7th world empire. Revelation 17:10, *"And there are seven kings: five are fallen* (Egypt, Assyria, Babylon, Medo-Persia, Greece), *and one is* (Rome, at the time that John wrote Revelation on Patmos) *and the other is not yet come; and when he cometh, he must continue a short space."* Here John writes about the seven empires of the world, and when he says, "the other is not yet come, and when he cometh he must continue a short space," John points to this 7th world empire that will not last long. John said it "must continue a short space."

It is the European Union of to-day, but will ultimately be taken over by the final ruler, the anti-christ, as in Revelation 17:11, *"And the beast* (the anti-christ) *that was, and is not, even he* (the anti-christ) *is the eighth, and is of the seven* (the seven world empires), *and goeth into perdition."* The anti-christ will come to his end, as in 2 Thessalonians 2:8, *"...that Wicked be revealed, whom the Lord shall consume with the spirit of His mouth, and shall destroy with the brightness of His coming."* Revelation 17:12 confirms what we have just mentioned, that the ten horns are ten kings, *"And the ten horns which thou sawest are ten kings, which have received no kingdom as yet, but receive power as kings one hour with the beast.* (the anti-christ*) 13. These have one mind, and shall give their power and strength unto the beast."* This verse 12 is so easy to understand. The ten horns, or the ten kings, from this 7th empire, will give all their support to the anti-christ. The ten horns from Revelation 13:1 are the same as the ten toes from Daniel 2:42, *"And as the toes of the feet were part of iron, and part of clay, so the kingdom shall be partly strong, and partly broken."*

It should be clear from this that the ten horns and the ten toes are both pointing to the final ten kings from the 7th world empire which the anti-christ takes over for a short time until he comes to his end.

Revelation 13:5, *"And there was given him a mouth speaking great things and blasphemies; and power was given unto him to continue forty and two months."* Here the anti-christ is blaspheming God, yet power was given to him for forty-two months, which is 3 ½ years. Daniel speaks about the final 3 ½ years of the great tribulation in chapter 12:6, *"How long shall it be to the end of these wonders? 7...and sware by him that liveth forever that it shall be for a time* (a year*), times* (two years), *and an half* (half a year*);"* the same total of 3 ½ years. Also, in Daniel 7:25, *"And he shall speak great words against the most High* (Jesus Christ*), and shall wear out the saints of the most High, and think to change times and laws: and they shall be given into his hand until a time* (a year), *and times (two years), and the dividing of time* (half a year)*";* again for a total of 3 ½ years.

Why is it that Amillennialist do not believe that this last 3 ½ year period of the tribulation will be so terrible, with the anti-christ in power, as is clearly shown in Daniel and Revelation. Rev. Vander Waal says on page 75, "three and a half years after the rapture comes the tribulation, the time of great oppression. This is an axiom for Hal Lindsay. The talk of Babylon and the beast fits into this period. This axiom, too, must be rejected. It is thoroughly unscriptural."

Why would the Bible continue to mention this 3 ½ year period if it were not true? God's word continues to point out in Revelation 13:6, *"And he opened his mouth in blasphemy against God, to blaspheme His name, and His tabernacle and them that dwell in heaven. 7. And it was given unto him to make war with the saints, and to overcome them: and power was given him over all kindreds, and tongues, and nations."* It is very clear from this verse, that the anti-christ will rule the whole world with such power that he believes himself to be as God, and so, blasphemes the one true God.

2 Thessalonians 2:3-8 says that he will not be revealed and all of this will not happen until after Jesus has taken His believers to heaven in the rapture. *"Let no man deceive you by any means: for that day shall not come, except there come a falling away first, and that man of sin be revealed, the son of perdition; 4. Who opposeth and exalteth himself above all that is called God, or that is worshipped; so that he as God sitteth in the temple of God, showing himself that he is God. 6. And now ye know what withholdeth that he might be revealed in his time. 7...only he that letteth will let, until he* (the Holy Spirit) *be taken out of the way. 8. And then shall that Wicked be revealed, whom the Lord shall consume with the spirit of His mouth..."* Paul tells us that the Holy Spirit, in the body of believers, the church, is preventing the anti-christ from being revealed. When the church is raptured, the Holy Spirit will no longer be present upon the earth. Wickedness will go unrestrained on earth, and the time will be right for the anti-christ to then make his appearance. Again, this makes it very clear that the anti-christ has not yet begun his reign on earth.

"And I saw one of his heads as it were wounded to death; and his deadly wound was healed: and all the world wondered after the beast. 4. And they worshipped the dragon which gave power unto the beast, saying, Who is able to make war with him? 5. And there was given unto him a mouth speaking great things and blasphemies; and power was given unto

him to continue forty and two months. 6. And he opened his mouth in blasphemy against God, to blaspheme His name, and His tabernacle, and them that dwell in heaven. 7. And it was given unto him to make war with the saints, and to overcome them: and power was given him over all kindreds, and tongues, and nations. 8. And all that dwell upon the earth shall worship him, whose names are not written in the book of life of the Lamb slain from the foundation of the world. 9. If any man hath an ear, let him hear." Revelation 13:3-9

Verse 7 says that the anti-christ, after having been healed miraculously from a deadly wound, will be worshipped by the whole world. Then, for 3 ½ years the anti-christ will powerfully persecute the Jewish and Gentile tribulation saints, that have not been raptured, and are now exposed to the anti-christ's satanic powers. Matthew 24:21, *"For then* (in the latter days) *shall be great tribulation, such as was not since the beginning of the world to this time, no, nor ever shall be."* After reading these passages from scripture, could we possibly not take this seriously or literally, as to how bad it will be during the 'great' tribulation? Matthew 24:9 says, *"Then shall they deliver you up to be afflicted and shall kill you: and ye shall be hated of all nations for my name's sake. 10. And then shall many be offended, and shall betray one another, and shall hate one another."*

The same is mentioned in Luke 21:16, *"And ye shall be betrayed both by parents, and brethren, and kinsfolks, and friends, and some of you shall they cause to be put to death."* If we watch today's news carefully, we can see how close we have come to all this, as we hear that parents have murdered their children in cold blood, and children have murdered their parents. Not just one isolated case, but it is happening far too often at present, and all over. We know that this is all pointing towards the last days, as written in Matthew 24:14, *"And this gospel of the kingdom shall be preached in all the world for a witness unto all nations, and then shall the end come."* This passage shows how close we are to the end time, as the gospel is now preached in almost all nations on earth. We must therefore continue to preach the gospel to the few nations left in the world that have not yet heard the gospel of Jesus Christ.

Personally, we fully support the Van Impe Ministry that is presently preaching the gospel in 211 countries and has started television broadcasts on another 101 late night stations since January 2006, to reach more people between midnight and 6:00 am.

Matthew 24:14 says, *"and then shall the end come."* Then Jesus will set up His kingdom on the new earth as in Daniel 2:44, *"And in the days of these kings shall the God of heaven set up a kingdom, which shall never be destroyed: and the kingdom shall not be left to other people, but it shall break in pieces and consume all these kingdoms, and it shall stand forever."* Daniel refers here to the ten kings from Revelation 17:12, *"And the ten horns which thou sawest are ten kings, which have received no kingdom as yet; but receive power as kings one hour with the beast* (the anti-christ)*"* However, before this happens, Revelation 13:8 says, *"And all that dwell upon the earth shall worship him* (the anti-christ), *whose names are not written in the book of life of the lamb slain from the foundation of the world. 9. If any man have an ear, let him hear."* It is clear from verse 8 that the whole world will worship this beast (the anti-christ), everyone whose names are not written in the book of life. And then it says in verse 9, *"If any man have an ear, let him hear."* But do we really hear? Do we really understand what the apostle John is saying here? Who is this beast? Is it the anti-christ that will be revealed after the rapture?

Rev. Verbrugge says in his sermons about Revelation, "The 'beast' is every person and nation against Christ, that opposes Jesus Christ. The 'beast' is now. Not in the future. Not in the end time. The world we live in now is the beast!"

Why is it, that Amillennialist do not believe in a terrible "end time" as Jesus so clearly mentions in Matthew 24:21, *"For then* (the time just before Jesus returns) *shall be great tribulation such as was not since the beginning of the world to this time, no, nor, ever shall be."* How can one interpret this as if it does not point to the end time? Jesus says clearly, "Such as was not since the beginning of the world, no, nor ever shall be." In other words, when this great tribulation has come, there will not be any other after that. This could therefore not mean, as Verbrugge says, "The beast is not in the future, not in the end time. The world we live in now is the beast."

Rev. Vander Waal says on page 75 of his book, "Three and a half years after the rapture comes the tribulation, the time of great oppression. This is an axiom for Hal Lindsey. The talk of Babylon and the beast fits into this period. This axiom too, must be rejected. It is thoroughly unscriptural." Then on page 83 he says, "His conceptions about biblical prophecy lead to misunderstandings in the area of exegesis. When Daniel 12 talks about the 'time of the end' (vs.4 and 9) some translations and interpretations turn this into the 'end time'." (Why? Is there a difference between "time of the end" and "end time"?) He continues with, "This in turn fosters the notion that Daniel's visions deal with the absolute end of history. Thus his prophecies are not read as pointing to the events in the days of Antiochus Epiphanes, who ruled 175-164 BC, but as portraying events at the very end of time. The expression 'the last days' which is used by some of the other prophets, has furthered the same misconception."

Here we see again that the Amillennialist do not believe in a special end time, as Jesus so clearly has said. His remark, "The expression 'the last days' which is used by some of the other prophets has furthered the same misconception," is totally out of line. Almost all the other prophets, as well as the apostles have used the expression "the last days," in reference to the time just before the Lord's return. This raises the question, <u>Could they all be wrong</u>? Could they all have the same "Misconception"? Could it be possible, that all these prophets as well as the apostles were wrong, when they prophesied that these things would happen in "the last days," just before Jesus returns? Jesus Himself says in Matthew 24:33, *"...likewise ye, when you shall see all these things, know that it is near, even at the doors."* Jesus was answering a very specific question. Matthew 24:3 is very simple; *"And as He sat upon the Mount of Olives, the disciples came to Him privately, saying, Tell us, when shall these things be? And what shall be the sign of thy coming, <u>and of the end of the world?</u>"*

In Matthew 24, Mark 13 and Luke 21, Jesus tells us that when we will see all these things coming to pass simultaneously, we will know that his return is near, even at the doors. Let us therefore not believe that the prophets, "have futhered the same misconception", but instead believe what the apostle Peter says in 2 Peter 1:19, *"We have also a more sure word of prophecy; whereunto ye do well that ye take heed* (take it seriously), *as unto a light that shineth in a dark place, until the day dawn, and the day star arise in your hearts: 20. Knowing this first, that no prophecy of the scripture is of any private interpretation, 21. For prophecy came not in old time by the will of man: but holy men of God spake as they were moved by the Holy Ghost."*

Chapter 12

"Here is wisdom. Let him that hath understanding count the number of the beast: for it is the number of a man..."
Revelation 13:18

—ɷ—

Revelation 13:11, *"And I beheld another beast coming up out of the earth; and he had two horns like a lamb, and he spake as a dragon."* This second beast out of the earth is a symbol of religious power, the false prophet, the anti-christ's right hand, so to speak. Rev. 13:12; *"And he exerciseth all the power of the first beast* (the anti-christ) *before him, and causeth the earth and them which dwell therin to worship the first beast* (the anti-christ), *whose deadly wound has been healed."* It is clear from this verse that the second beast makes the whole earth to worship the first beast (the anti-christ). Revelation 13:13, *"And he doeth great wonders, so that he maketh fire come down from heaven on the earth in the sight of men, 14. And deceiveth them that dwell on the earth by means of those miracles which he had power to do in the sight of the beast* (the anti-christ); *saying to them that dwell on the earth, that they should make an image to the beast* (the anti-christ), *which had the wound by a sword, and did live."*

Here we see, that this second beast, the false prophet, is making an image of the first beast (the anti-christ) and that every one that does not worship this image will be killed. This passage from scripture shows how bad it will get during the tribulation for the people that have not been raptured by Jesus Christ. It makes it difficult to believe that all believers would have to go through the tribulation time, and that there would be no rapture, as the Amillennialist say.

Revelation 13:15, *"And he had power to give life unto the image of the beast, that the image of the beast should both speak, and cause that as many as would not worship the image of the beast should be killed."*

So anyone who does not worship the anti-christ, or his image, will be put to death. We also see, from verse 14 and 15, that the image the false prophet creates of the first beast (the anti-christ), is able to speak. We don't know if this is going to be a robot or a clone but either is possible, or almost possible, very soon, for the first time in history. The fact that anyone who does not worship this image will be killed, shows us how close we are to the tribulation time.

Revelation 13:16, *"And he* (the false prophet) *causeth all, both small and great, rich and poor, free and bond, to receive a mark in their right hand, or in their foreheads: 17. And that no man might buy or sell save he that had the mark, or the name of the beast, or the number of his name. 18. Here is wisdom, let him that hath understanding count the number of the beast: for it is the number of a man; and his number is six hundred threescore and six."* For the first time in history, it is possible that this prophecy could be fulfilled, soon in fact. Scientists have developed a tiny computer chip, that could be inserted beneath the skin, to hold complete financial, health, and identification records, so that the anti-christ could keep track of all humans on earth, as in Rev. 13:17, *"And that no man might buy or sell, save he that had the mark, or the name of the beast, or the number of his name."* It is clear from verse 17, that no one on earth can buy or sell unless one has the mark of the beast. Believers have already been raptured, and will not have to go through this. However, those that have been left behind that refuse the mark will be killed.

Verse 18 says, *"Here is wisdom. Let him that hath understanding count the number of the beast: for it is the number of a man; and his number is Six hundred threescore and six."* This tells us that it will be a man, a person, and not, as Rev. Verbrugge says, "666 is a false imitation of the Holy Spirit." Why can we not just read what God's word says? The Bible says, *"Here is wisdom ... for it is the number of a man."*

What is stated here in Revelation 13 verses 17 and 18 has never been possible until now. Computers can make trillions of calculations per second, fast enough to give the anti-christ the ability to control anyone who would buy or sell throughout the whole world. The implant under the skin combined with the instant calculation from the computer would eliminate the necessity of money. All financial transactions (buying and selling) would only be possible with the computer chip. This would easily prepare the way for implementation of the mark of the beast — 666. This computer chip has already been in use for some time in animals to keep track of them. Through the information on the microchip implanted under the skin, the anti-christ could keep track of, and control, all the inhabitants of the earth, as described in Rev. 13:17. Already 'Digital Angel' in West Palm Beach, Florida, is getting ready for the microchip for humans.

Daniel 12:4 says, *"But thou O Daniel, shut up the words, and seal the book, even to the time of the end: many shall run to and fro, and knowledge shall be increased."* Notice what Daniel says here, "Knowledge shall be increased." We must be getting close to the time of the end, because today, knowledge is increased beyond what the human mind could even comprehend in Daniel's day. Today anyone can know almost anything on any subject instantly, with the Internet and a few keystrokes. Already, 'Echelon Network' in England, can make 3 trillion calculations per second, while Japan has increased this to 13 trillion calculations per second. China is presently working to make 1000 trillion calculations per second.

Daniel also says here in verse 4 "that many shall run to and fro." People are traveling today, to destinations anywhere on the globe, like never before in history. Within any city or large metropolitan area, the number of people hustling from place to place, whether in cars, or on transit, or even on foot, is unprecedented. Imagine if Daniel had been shown a vision of today's rush hour. "Many shall rush to and fro," is a pretty accurate description, and it indicates we are near "the time of the end."

Until today, Revelation 13:17 was difficult to understand, which is why Daniel 12:4 says, *"seal the book, even to the time of the end."* And again in verses 9 and 10 Daniel says, *"for the words are closed up and sealed till the time of the end. 10. Many shall be purified, and made white, and tried; and the wicked shall do wickedly: but none of the wicked shall understand; but the wise shall understand."* We can see now, how easy it will be for the anti-christ to control the whole earth with his mark, the mark of the beast, 666. Although this description of 666 is so easy to understand for our time, yet Rev. Verbrugge says, "The mark in their forehead is symbolic," Webster's dictionary says, "The use of symbols to represent invisible, intangible or abstract things." Why do Amillennialist call so many passages of scripture 'symbolic' meaning invisible, intangible or abstract?

This chapter 13 of Revelation clearly describes the end time, when this 666 will be revealed. As Daniel talks about the end time in Daniel 12:8, *"...then said I, O my Lord, what shall be the end of these things? 9. And He said, Go thy way, Daniel: for the words are closed up and sealed till the time of the end."* We know that Daniel is talking here about the last days, just before Jesus returns, because Daniel 12:1 says,

"And at that time shall Michael stand up, the great prince which standeth for the children of thy people: and there shall be a time of trouble, such as never was since there was a nation, even to that same time: and at that time thy people shall be delivered, everyone that shall be found written in the book." It is very difficult to imagine how anyone could not take this passage from scripture literally. Jesus says the same words in Matthew 24:21, *"For then shall be great tribulation, such as was not since the beginning of the world to this time* (the time Jesus will return) *no, nor, ever shall be."*

How can we interpret this as symbolic? John in Revelation reiterates what Jesus had spoken previously in Matthew 24:21. He points to the terrible time that will happen on earth, as described in Revelation 13:5-8, where the beast, the anti-christ's false prophet, has been given power over all kindreds, and tongues, and nations.

He will start a new world order, run by a world dictator, the anti-christ, as has actually been proposed already by several heads of state during the past years. In 1983, Henry Spaak, who at that time was responsible for the start-up of the European Union, said, "We need a man that can control the whole world. Be he God or the devil, we will receive him." This promise of Spaak might be fulfilled soon. The anti-christ will rule the whole world, with the new world order, as prophesied in Daniel 7:23, *"Thus He said, The fourth beast shall be the fourth kingdom upon earth* (the revised Roman Empire, the European Union) *... and shall devour the whole earth, and shall tread it down, and break it in pieces."* We know that when this happens, Jesus will return soon, because verse 26 says, *"But the judgment shall sit, and they shall take away his* (the anti-christ's) *dominion, to consume and to destroy it unto the end."*

When Revelation 13 says that the beast is blaspheming God and saying, "I am God," we can see that this is already happening today within the "New Age Movement." They

127

say, "We do not need Christ" and "I am God." They misuse the "Father title" of "I am", as in Exodus 3:13-14, *"And Moses said unto God, Behold, when I come unto the children of Israel, and shall say unto them, The God of your fathers hath sent me unto you; and they shall say to me, What is His name? what shall I say unto them? 14. And God said unto Moses, I AM THAT I AM: and He said, Thus shalt thou say unto the children of Israel, I AM hath sent me unto you."*

Chapter 13

"And when the thousand years are expired, Satan shall be loosed out of his prison." Revelation 20:7

—⁓—

R evelation 20:1, *"And I saw an angel come down from heaven, having the key of the bottomless pit and a great chain in his hand. 2. And he laid hold on the dragon, that old serpent, which is the Devil and Satan, and bound him a thousand years, 3. And cast him into the bottomless pit, and shut him up, and set a seal upon him, that he should deceive the nations no more, till the thousand years should be fulfilled: and after that he must be loosed a little season. 4. And I saw thrones, and they sat upon them, and judgment was given unto them."*

It is clear from these scripture passages, that Satan will not be bound, until Jesus is about to return, because verse 4 says, *"I saw thrones and they sat upon them, and judgment was given unto them,"* indicating resurrection day had come. Revelation 20:11, *"And I saw a great white throne, and Him that sat on it."* (Jesus) This makes it very clear that Satan will not be bound till Jesus sits on the white throne. Dispensationalist therefore, read Rev. 20:1-4 literally, as God's word says it. Amillennialist however do not take this literally as Rev. Hoekema says in CRC Viewpoint, "How do Amillennialist interpret the binding of Satan described in Revelation 20:1-3? We believe that Satan was bound by Christ at the beginning of Christ's earthly ministry. Note for example, that when Jesus was accused of casting out demons by the power of Satan, he replied, 'How can one enter into a strong man's house and plunder his goods, unless he first binds the strong man?' (Matthew 12:29 RSV) This binding of Satan means that during the gospel age, Satan is kept from 'deceiving the nations.' (Rev. 20:3) In other words, during this age, Satan cannot totally prevent the spread of the gospel, nor can he gather Christ's enemies together to attack the church,"

How can we assume that when Jesus said in Matthew 12:29, *"Or else how can one enter into a strong man's house, and spoil his goods except he first bind the strong man and then he will spoil his house,"* that this meant He would bind Satan at the time of His earthly ministry? Jesus did not really say here, that He would bind Satan at that time. How could Satan have tempted Jesus, if he was already bound? However, He does literally say that Satan would be bound for a thousand years at the time of His return, in Revelation 20:1-3, *"And he laid hold on the dragon, that old serpent, which is the devil, and Satan, and bound him a thousand years."* Jesus did say this literally because He told John to write this in Rev. 20:1-3 and since Revelation 1:1 says, *"The Revelation of Jesus Christ, which God gave unto him..."* (John), we can take it literally, that Jesus said that Satan would be bound for a thousand years at the time of Jesus return, and not at the time of His earthly ministry. This shows that the Amillennialist interpretation of Matthew 12:29 does not reflect the proper interpretation.

There is also another reason why Satan could not have been bound before Jesus' return to the new earth. Revelation 12:12 says, *"Therefore rejoice, ye heavens, and ye that dwell in them. Woe to the inhabiters of the earth and of the sea! for the devil is come down unto you, having great wrath, because he knoweth that he hath but a short time.* " How could Satan have been bound earlier during Christ's earthly ministry, and remain bound until Jesus returns, when 2 Peter 5:8 tell us to, *"Be sober, be vigilant; because your adversary the devil, as a roaring lion, walketh about seeking whom he may devour."* That doesn't sound to me as though he's bound. We do know that Rev. 12:12 points to the time of Jesus return, because it says, *"he knoweth that he hath but a short time."*

"Having great wrath," means he will cause terrible things to happen on earth, as Jesus said in Matthew 24:21, *"For then shall be great tribulation, such as was not from the beginning of the world to this time, no, nor ever shall be."* There will be no greater tribulation again.

Yet Rev. Hoekema says in CRC Viewpoint, "Nor can he (Satan) gather Christ's enemies together to attack the church." How can he justify this with all the passages from scripture that warn us about Armageddon? We will discuss this in the next chapter.

I do not understand why Amillennialist do not want to hear about anything bad that will happen before Jesus returns? Rev. Hoekema says in CRC Viewpoint, "this binding of Satan means that during the gospel age Satan is kept from deceiving the nations." How do I interpret this with Revelation 12:12? *"Therefore rejoice, ye heavens and ye that dwell in them. Woe to the inhabiters of the earth and of the sea! for the devil is come down unto you, having great wrath, because he knoweth that he hath but a short time."* Having great wrath is showing the opposite of "Kept from deceiving the nations," as Hoekema says. How can he say this, as Rev 20:8 clearly says, *"And shall go out to deceive the nations which are in four quarters of the earth..."?*

There is also one more reason why Satan could not have been bound at Christ's earthly ministry, because Rev. 20:10 says, *"And the devil that deceived them was cast into the lake*

131

of fire and brimstone, where the beast and the false prophet are, and shall be tormented day and night forever." This passage from scripture says that when Satan is cast into the lake of fire, the beast and the false prophet are already there. In fact, they have already been there for a thousand years. We know from Rev. 19:20, *"And the beast was taken, and with him the false prophet that wrought miracles before him, with which he deceived them that had received the mark of the beast, and them that worshipped his image. These both were cast alive into the lake of fire burning with brimstone,"*

The beast and the false prophet were cast into the lake of fire in Revelation 19:20, and then in Rev. 20:1-3 Satan is bound for the next thousand years and cast into the bottomless pit. Then in Rev. 20:7 Satan is loosed again after the thousand years are expired, and finally, in Rev. 20:10, Satan is cast into the same lake of fire where the beast and false prophet are. There is a thousand year difference between the time when the beast and the false prophet are cast into the lake of fire, and when Satan is cast into the same lake of fire. That's about as clear and concise as it could possibly be, indicating that there will indeed be a thousand year millennium. Jesus says so here very clearly, through the apostle John.

I described in detail how clear God's word is if we take it literally, as Jesus has intended us to do, I am sure, and not symbolically, as the Amillennialist say we should. As I have mentioned earlier in previous chapters, the reason that I am writing this book is to request of the CRC Church at Calvin Seminary, that if any member of any Christian Reformed Church would want to interpret God's word literally, as dispensationalists do, they should not be "deposed," as Rev. Hoekema says in CRC Viewpoint, "The Reverend Mr. H Bultema, then pastor of the first Christian Reformed Church of Muskegan, Michigan, published a book entitled 'Maranatha' in which he defended the dispensational position. The Christian Reformed Synod, after examining

Bultema's views, found him to be in conflict with the creeds on two points ...since Bultema did not retract these views, he was deposed." Hoekema also says, "D. H. Kromminga, a professor at Calvin Seminary, recognized that his premillennial views were in conflict with article 37 of the Belgic Confession ...appealed to Synod for a judgment regarding the scriptural validity of his article, but he died before the matter could be resolved."

I am vehemently against anyone being "deposed" or shall we say being "kicked out of the church" for interpreting God's word literally. Nowhere can I find in the Bible that we cannot interpret God's word literally. Instead the apostle Peter says in 2 Peter 1:19, *"We have also a more sure word of prophecy..."* If a word is sure, then should we not therefore take it literally? If a member defends the dispensational position, or in other words interprets the scriptures literally, why can we not discuss this matter as brothers and sisters in Christ, in the light of God's word, (as I have tried to do in my book) instead of that member being "deposed?" Then if a member insists that he or she believes that a literal interpretation is correct, so be it, and that member should not have to leave the church for that reason, but should instead be able to stay if so desired.

Chapter 14

"And he gathered them together into a place called in the Hebrew tongue Armageddon" Revelation 16:16

—ɯ—

Revelation 16:14, *"For they are the spirits of devils, working miracles, which go forth unto the kings of the earth and of the whole world, to gather them to the battle of that great day of God Almighty."* Here God's word calls the battle of Armageddon the battle of the great day of God Almighty, and as Rev. 16:16 says, *"And he gathered them together into a place called in the Hebrew tongue Armageddon."* The apostle John says here that the whole world will be involved in this 'great' battle, as it says in Zechariah 14:1, *"Behold, the day of the Lord cometh, and thy spoil shall be divided in the midst of thee. 2. For I will gather all nations against Jerusalem to battle, and the city shall be taken, and the houses rifled, and the women ravished; and half of the city shall go forth into captivity, and the residue of the people shall not be cut off from the city."* Zechariah says here, that Jerusalem will be taken when all nations come up against the city, and some of the inhabitants will go into captivity, while some will stay. The Bible does not say how long the battle will be, or how long those people will go into captivity. However, the Bible makes it clear that the Lord will come to the rescue, as in Zechariah 14:3, *"Then shall the Lord go forth, and fight against those nations, as when He fought in the day of battle."* We see that all through the Bible the Lord foretold that Armageddon would come. Yet, the Amillennialist cannot believe that anything out of the ordinary will happen. Rev. Verbrugge says, "Armageddon, the final battle, is not a battle with machineguns, but a battle for the word of God, because salvation has come." How can he say this? We just have read in Revelation 16 and in Zechariah, about how bad it will get because of the terrible warfare.

It seems as though they just do not take Armageddon seriously, as Vander Waal says in his book on page 130, "Covenant judgment is turned into secularized ruin and wrath. No one is surprised to hear Churchill talking about the 'vials of wrath' or to see Leon Uris borrowing the name 'Armageddon' for his book about the cold war in Berlin. Apocalyptic language is common property; it is part of our culture. Christians who are looking for popularity join in the game. Success is assured, for everyone loves a good scare… 131… therefore people seize on the book of Revelation as a platform on which to build their wild fantasies about the future… The book of Revelation is not a 'Handbook to the future' or a political almanac."

He continues with, "People have always been interested in manmade apocalypticism. Today there is a modern apocalypticism in a variety of forms e.g. the gruesome predictions about the imminent destruction of the world through atom bombs. Such apocalypticism has little to do with the gospel; the resemblance is purely superficial,"

How can he say this? If one reads Joel 2:3, *"A fire devoureth before them; and behind them a flame burneth; the land is as the garden of Eden before them, and behind them a desolate wilderness; yea, and nothing shall escape them."* Does this not clearly resemble atomic warfare? It is also described in many more places in scripture, such as in Revelation 9:18,

"By these three was the third part of men killed, by the fire, and by the smoke, and by the brimstone, which issued out of their mouth," and in Zechariah 14:12, where the heat radiation of a nuclear blast is described with remarkable accuracy, *"And this shall be the plague wherewith the Lord shall smite all the people that have fought against Jerusalem; Their flesh shall consume away while they stand upon their feet, and their eyes shall consume away in their holes, and their tongue shall consume away in their mouth."*

The Lord refers to "Brimstone" many times, as in Revelation 14:10, *"The same shall drink of the wine of the wrath of God, which is poured out without mixture into the cup of His indignation; and he* (the beast, the anti-christ) *shall be tormented with 'fire and brimstone' in the presence of the Holy angels, and in the presence of the Lamb:"* The Bible is full of "apocalypticism" as Vander Waal calls it. He calls it "manmade" which does not accurately describe the terrible punishment the Lord will bring at the time of Armageddon, as in Ezekiel 38:22, *"And I will plead against him with pestilence and with blood; and I will rain upon him* (the enemies that attack Israel), *and upon his bands, and upon the many people that are with him, an overflowing rain, and 'great' hailstones, fire, and brimstone."* How can anyone call this "manmade apocalypticism" as the Bible tells us clearly that these prophecies are from the Lord?

The apostle Peter says in 2 Peter 1:19, *"We have also a more sure word of prophecy... 20. Knowing this first, that no prophecy of the scripture is of any private interpretation. 21. For the prophecy came not in old time by the will of man: but holy men of old spake as they were moved by the Holy Ghost,"* Since there are prophecies all through the Bible that point to "Armageddon" we can be sure therefore that, "we have also a more sure word of prophecy."

Isaiah 66:15, *"For, Behold, the Lord will come with fire, and with His chariots like a whirlwind, to render His anger with fury, and His rebuke with flames of fire. 16. For by fire and by His sword will the Lord plead with all flesh: and the slain of the Lord shall be many."* Verse 16 says, "and the slain of the Lord shall be many." This shows that it will not be a "manmade apocalypticism," but punishment from the Lord for the iniquity of the world, as in Joel 2:1, *"Blow ye the trumpet, in Zion, and sound an alarm in my holy mountain: let all the inhabitants of the land tremble: for the day of the Lord cometh, for it is nigh at hand. 2. A day of darkness and of gloominess, a day of clouds and of thick darkness."*

We know that Joel is talking here about the "last days" because verse 10 says, *"The earth shall quake before them; the heavens shall tremble: the sun and the moon shall be dark, and the stars shall withdraw their shining."* Joel 2:30 says, *"And I will show wonders in the heavens and in the earth, blood, and fire, and pillars of smoke."* Again, describing the exact signs of atomic warfare. Also in Obadiah 1:15, we read, *"For the day of the Lord is near upon all the heathen:"* And in Micah 1:3, *"For, behold, the Lord cometh forth out of His place, and will come down, and tread upon the high places of the earth. 4. And the mountains shall be molten under Him, and the valleys shall be cleft, as wax before the fire."*

How many more times does the Lord have to tell us that "Armageddon" is real? Not a "manmade apocalypticism" but a terrible punishment from the Lord for the iniquity of this world. Read again Zephaniah 1:2, *"I will utterly consume all things from off the land, saith the Lord. 3. I will consume man and beast; I will consume the fowls of the heavens, and the fishes of the sea... 14. The great day of the Lord is near, it is near, and hasteth greatly, even the voice of the day of the Lord: the mighty man shall cry there bitterly. 15. That day is a day of wrath, a day of trouble and distress, a day of wasteness and desolation... 17. And I will bring distress upon men, that they shall walk like blind men, because they have sinned against the Lord.*" Clearly this is not a "manmade apocalypticism," but a punishment from the Lord.

How can Amillennialist not take this serious, and not believe in a 7 year tribulation time, with Armageddon, but just think that everything will continue the same until Jesus returns? The apostle Peter says in 2 Peter 3:3, *"Knowing this first, that there shall come in the last days scoffers, walking after their own lusts, 4. And saying, Where is the promise of His coming? for since the fathers fell asleep, all things continue as they were from the beginning of the creation. 5. For this they willingly are ignorant of, that by the word of God the heavens were of old, and the earth standing out of the water and in the water: 6. Whereby the world that then was, being overflowed with water, perished: 7. But the heavens and the earth, which are now, by the same word are kept in store, reserved unto fire against the day of judgment and perdition of ungodly men... 12. Looking for and hasting unto the coming of the day of God, wherein the heavens being on fire shall be dissolved and the elements shall melt with fervent heat."*

This verse 12 is the closest description yet of an atomic war, as it says, "the elements shall melt with fervent heat." Also, anyone that does not believe in a terrible judgment day of the Lord, with a real battle of Armageddon, (as the Amillennialist mentioned previously) should read again 2 Peter 3 verses 6 and 7, where the Lord says, that as sure as the world in Noah's time was punished by the flood, so surely has the Lord kept the heavens and the earth, which are now, in store for punishment by fire in the judgment day of the Lord. And as surely as the flood that destroyed the earth in Noah's time is to be taken literally, so too must we also realize that the fire, and the Day of Judgment, are to be taken literally as well!

It is absolutely clear that "Armageddon" will not be a "manmade apocalypticism" but is a "Judgment Day" of the

Lord. Zechariah says in 12:2, *"Behold, I will make Jerusalem a cup of trembling unto all the people round about, when they shall be in the siege both against Judah and against Jerusalem. 3. And in that day will I make Jerusalem a burdensome stone for all the people: all that burden themselves with it shall be cut in pieces, though all the people of the earth be gathered together against it."* It is again clear from this verse that all nations come against Jerusalem to do battle.

Revelation speaks of Armageddon also in Rev. 14:7, *"Saying with a loud voice, Fear God and give glory to Him; for the hour of His judgment is come: and worship Him that made heaven, and earth, and the sea, and the fountains of waters."* Here John talks about "the hour of judgment" (Armageddon).

In all these books of the Bible, the prophets have said that the Lord's judgment, Armageddon, would come upon all the world, during the last 3 ½ years of the tribulation, the "great" tribulation. Jesus says in Matthew 24:21 that He will return at the end of the battle of Armageddon. *"And His feet shall stand in that day upon the Mount of Olives"* Zechariah 14:4.

And still, in spite of all these prophecies, Amillennialist believe that there will not be an Armageddon. They still believe that the Lord will not punish this world through His "hour of judgment." Rev. Verbrugge says, "Armageddon, the final battle, is not a battle with machine guns, but a battle for the word of God, because salvation has come." However, scripture clearly says that there will be a physical battle, not only with machine guns, but much, much worse. The way Revelation describes it, only after this terrible battle with atomic warfare, will "salvation" come, and not during, or before, this battle of Armageddon.

Rev. Vander Waal also has a totally different view of Armageddon, as he says in his book on page 130, "No one is surprised to hear Churchill talking about the 'vials of wrath' or to see Leon Uris borrowing the name 'Armageddon' for the book about the cold war in Berlin. Christians who are looking for popularity join in on the game. Success is assured, for everyone loves a good scare." What a way to describe "Armageddon." To make fun of it, as if it were not a judgment from the Lord, which could come very soon as we are seeing the signs, which Jesus foretold in Matthew 24.

No wonder Vander Waal says, "People have always been interested in 'Man made Apocalypticism'," and on page 129, "What do I get out of it?" He continues with, " 'Surely I am coming soon,' Jesus says at the end of the book. How can that assurance be reconciled with the passage of nineteen centuries since then? Defenders of the futuristic interpretation have to perform exegetical acrobatics to get around that problem." Actually, we the defenders of "the futuristic interpretations" do not have to perform "exegetical acrobatics" to get around this problem, because it is not a problem at all. Indeed Jesus says in Rev. 22:7 and 22:12 *"Behold, I come quickly."* Also, Revelation 1:1 says, *"The Revelation of Jesus Christ, which God gave unto him, to show unto his servants things which must shortly come to pass."* As well as in Rev. 1:3, *"Blessed is he that readeth, and they that hear the words of this prophesy, and keep those things that are written therein, for the time is at hand."*

Although Jesus said several times here, "Behold I come quickly," and "the time is at hand", that is no reason for Vander Waal to say that we who believe in a "Futuristic Interpretation" have to come up with an interpretation to explain why it has taken almost 2000 years since Jesus said, "I am coming soon", and "the time is at hand." I am sure that the apostle John was aware of Jesus' words which he had given to us so we would know when His coming was near, as in Luke 21:24, *"and Jerusalem will be trodden down by the gentiles, until the time of the gentiles be fulfilled."* It was not until 1967, when Jerusalem for the first time in nearly 2500 years, was again in Jewish hands, as the prophets had foretold would happen in the latter days. Now Luke 21:24 had been fulfilled. The apostle John when he wrote Revelation in AD 90-96 on the Island of Patmos, did not know, (as nobody did) at what time Luke 21:24 would be fulfilled, and since the Lord says, "a day is as a thousand years and a thousand years is as a day," Jesus saying "I come quickly," could have happened a year after John wrote Revelation, or as we know, has not happened yet in almost 2000 years. Therefore it is all so clear if one reads God's word literally (as I'm sure the Lord has intended us to do.)

Vander Waal continues with, "But that's not all there is to be said in response. We could point to the Old Testament as well, where we also read about imminent judgments, judgments that have since come and gone." Why is it that Amillennialist will not believe that terrible judgments will come just before Jesus returns? They believe that all terrible judgments mentioned in scripture "have come and gone." The terrible judgments, as mentioned in previous chapters dealing with the anti-christ, the four horsemen, and Armageddon, have not "come and gone" yet, but are obviously very close, taking into consideration what is happening in the world today. That these "imminent judgments" will happen during the 3½ years of the Great Tribulation, and that "gruesome predictions" through atomic weapons, are clearly foretold in the Bible. As we have seen in previous chapters, these judgments could happen soon, now that Iran has atomic weapons. Iran - whose head of state said recently, "We will not rest till we have stopped Israel from being a nation." Exactly the same words as Psalm 83:4, where it says, *"They have said, Come, and let us cut them off from being a nation, that the name of Israel may no more be in remembrance."*

Why can we not take it seriously when Daniel, Ezekiel, and Matthew 24 clearly say that horrendous things will happen in the future, and not like Vander Waal says on the back cover of his book, "Hal Lindsay uses Biblical prophecy to open a supermarket in which he sells inside information about the near future, especially World War III. The sources of his information are the books of Daniel, Revelation, Ezekiel, and Matthew 24. There's no need to be uncertain about the future any longer." He is right about one thing, there is no need to be uncertain about the future because the Lord has foretold all that will happen in His Word, as we have seen in previous chapters, and we do not have to open a supermarket to get this information. Just open God's word and He will tell us the future, as He told the future to Nebuchadnezzar in Daniel 2:28, *"But there is a God in heaven that revealeth secrets, and maketh known to the king Nebuchadnezzar what shall be in the latter days ... 29. ... what should come to pass hereafter, and He that revealeth secrets maketh known to thee what shall come to pass."*

Why would our Lord tell Nebuchadnezzar what would happen in the "latter days" (which we know from scripture is just before Jesus returns) and why should we not know this if we read the book of Daniel? Is this the source of information to get in a "supermarket" as Vander Waal says? Why can we not take Daniel 2:28 literally when the Lord tells us what will happen in the future? Nebuchadnezzar did when he said in Daniel 2:47, *"The king answered unto Daniel and said, Of a truth it is, that your God is a God of gods, and a Lord of kings, and a revealer of secrets, seeing thou couldst reveal this secret."*

Here Nebuchadnezzar openly admits that God reveals secrets about the future, and yet we keep saying that the Bible is not a book foretelling the future. Vander Waal says on page 131, "The book of Revelation is not a 'Handbook to the future' or a political almanac." Not only Revelation, but Daniel and Ezekiel also, are "Handbooks to the future," if one wanted to call them that, because both Daniel and Ezekiel, as well as Revelation, refer to what Jesus said in Matthew 24 regarding what will happen in the future when the "great tribulation" starts. Similarly, in Ezekiel 38:14, *"Therefore son of man, prophesy and say unto Gog,* (Russia) *Thus saith the Lord God; in that day, when my people of Israel dwelleth safely, shalt thou not know it? 15. And thou* (Russia) *shalt come from thy place out of the north parts, thou, and many people with thee ... 16. And thou shalt come up against my people of Israel, as a cloud to cover the land; it shall be in the latter days, and I shall bring thee against my land, that the heathen may know me, when I shall be sanctified in thee, O Gog, before their eyes."*

Is it not amazing that the Lord says here, "and I shall bring thee against 'My' land"? The Lord himself says here that Israel is "My land." This must be an eye opener to anyone who still believes that the Lord has "dismissed" his people the Jews, as Vander Waal says on page 139 in his book, "Jesus shows us how the Lord finally dismisses Jerusalem, the city that slaughtered the Lamb. Henceforth he will no longer recognize the Jews as His people." Why would the Lord say that the land He promised to Abraham, is "My land," if He would dismiss the Jews as His people. Instead, we have seen, the Jews did come home again on May 14, 1948, but they will have to go through Armageddon yet as Ezekiel says in chapter 38:5, *"Persia, Ethiopia, and Libya with them* (Russia) *...8. After many days thou shalt be visited: in the latter years thou shalt come into the land that is brought back from the sword, and is gathered out of many people, against the mountains of Israel..."*

Ezekiel clearly says here that Israel will be invaded by many nations, as in Zechariah 14:2, *"For I will gather all nations against Jerusalem to battle, and the city shall be taken, and the houses rifled..."* However, Ezekiel also says that "in the latter years" it will happen, meaning just before the return of Jesus, as in Zechariah 14:4, *"And His feet shall stand in that day* (the day that all the nations come up against Jerusalem) *upon the Mount of Olives, which is before Jerusalem...*" The prophet Daniel also talks about Armageddon in Daniel 11:40, "*And at the time of the end* (the end of Armageddon) *shall the king of the south* (the combined Arabian countries) *push at him* (the anti-christ) *and the king of the north* (Russia) *shall come against him* (the anti-christ)..." Since the prophets Daniel and Ezekiel, the apostle Matthew, and the book of Revelation, speak about the same battle of "Armageddon," it is difficult not to believe how tremendous this battle will be. Also, in Daniel 11:44, "*But tidings out of the east* (the combined countries of the Orient) *and out of the north* (Russia) *shall trouble him* (the anti-christ): *therefore he* (the anti-christ) *shall go forth with great fury to destroy, and utterly to make away many.*" This passage shows that many countries will attack the anti-christ, and that the anti-christ in great anger, will destroy as much as possible.

Not only the armies from Russia, but also the armies from the Orient are coming towards Israel, where the anti-christ has set up his headquarters, as in Daniel 11:45, "*And he* (the anti-christ) *shall plant the tabernacles of his palace between the seas in the glorious holy mountain; yet he shall come to his end, and none shall help him.*" The anti-christ, we see here at the end of Armageddon, will come to his end, as in 2 Thessalonians 2:8, "*And then shall that Wicked be revealed* (the anti-christ*), whom the Lord shall consume with the spirit of his mouth, and shall destroy with the brightness of his coming.*" And in Zechariah 14:4 we read, "*And His feet will stand in that day upon the Mount of Olives.*"

Daniel 11:44 is not the only reference to the Oriental armies attacking Israel. This is again confirmed in Revelation 9:14, "*Saying to the sixth angel, which had the trumpet, Loose the four angels which are bound in the great river Euphrates. 15. And the four angels were loosed, which were prepared for an hour, and a day, and a month, and a year, for to slay the third part of men. 16. And the number of the army* (Oriental) *of the horsemen were two hundred thousand thousand;* (200 million) *and I heard the number of them."* Revelation 16:12 again refers to the same Oriental armies, *"And the sixth angel poured out his vial upon the great river Euphrates; and the water dried up, that the way of the kings of the East* (Orient) *might be prepared."*

How can anyone not take this literally, since it is mentioned by so many different prophets and written at different times, hundreds of years apart? It is clear from these passages of scripture that an army of 200,000,000 will come across the Euphrates River in Iraq against Israel, and that the Lord will dry up the Euphrates River so that this army can come across without any hindrance. Of course, Armageddon will finally come to an end as written in Ezekiel 39:8, *"Behold, it is come, and it is done, saith the Lord God; this is the day whereof I have spoken."*

However, before Armageddon will come to an end, when the 7 year tribulation is finished, many signs, which Jesus spoke of in Matthew 24, will be fulfilled. Matthew 24:37 says, *"For as the days of Noah were, so shall also the coming of the Son of man be."* We could compare Matthew 24:37 today with the blaspheming and insulting introduction of Dan Brown's "The Da Vinci Code"; first the book, and now the movie, where our Lord and Savior, Jesus Christ is more insulted and blasphemed against than ever before. What amazes me is that even Christians say that we should read the book, or see the movie; to find out what exactly it is all about. But we do not have to read the book, or see the movie to know how much trash it is. The media does a good job of informing us that it is about Jesus having had sex with Mary Magdalene, who then had a daughter, or possibly even more children from Jesus. Dan Brown's book and movie are therefore a direct attack against Jesus Christ, as well as against the church, because we know that Jesus is the Son of God, and without sin as God's Word clearly says.

Since "The Da Vinci Code" is such an insulting and blasphemous accusation against our Savior Jesus Christ, it should be boycotted as much as possible. I sincerely hope that ministers will clearly condemn this book, as well as the movie from their pulpits every Sunday, as does Jack Van Impe in all his programs. I appreciate it that he, in no uncertain terms, condemns this trash, as much as he possibly can by saying "the Da Vinci Code" is a satanic doctrine. We must stand up for Jesus in these perilous times, when this blaspheming, fraudulent movie insults our Savior Jesus Christ with this "all time 200 million block buster box office hit." The very fact that such a movie is a "blockbuster", shows how close we are to the return of Jesus, as He will not allow His Name to be insulted and blasphemed against for long, as He said in Matthew 24:37, *"As the days of Noah were, so shall also the coming of the Son of Man be."*

To understand how deceptive the "Da Vinci Code" is, read the book, "the Da Vinci Deception:" from Erwin W. Lutzer. Erwin W. Lutzer is senior pastor of the Moody Church in Chicago and does an excellent job of explaining why the Da Vinci Code is pure fabrication and deception.

At the council of Nicea in 325 AD it was confirmed that Christ was "God of every god." Yet today, we have the Gnostic Bible, which gives us permission to make God into whomever we want Him, (or her) to be. The Gnostic Bible tries to free us from "restricting doctrine" as they say, such as the Virgin Birth, the Deity of Christ, as well as Christ's resurrection; all things that believers in Christ accept as the truth of God's Word. The Gnostic gospels in the Da Vinci Code provide the basis for the alleged marriage of Jesus to Mary Magdalene, supposedly referring to the Gnostic Gospel of Philip. How totally ridiculous the Gnostic Gospels are is shown in the Gnostic Gospel of Thomas where it says, " Yeshua (Jesus) said unto them, when you make the two into one, and when you make the inner like the outer and the outer like the inner, and the upper like the lower, and when you make the male and the female into a single one, so that the male will not be the male, nor the female be female, when you make eyes in the place of an eye, and a hand in the place of a hand, a foot in the place of a foot, an image in the place of an image, then you will enter the kingdom."

Since these Gnostic gospels are frequently used in the Da Vinci Code, just how ridiculous and deceptive they are is shown from the above-mentioned Gospel of Thomas. Just compare the Gnostic Bible to our real Bible, being God's Word, as the apostle Luke tells us that he examined the scriptures thoroughly, to show that our Bible is truly God's Word. Luke says in Luke 1:1-4, *"Forasmuch as many have taken in hand to set forth in order a declaration of those things which are most surely believed among us. 2. Even as they delivered them unto us, which from the beginning were eyewitnesses, and ministers of the word; 3. It seemed good to me also, having had perfect understanding of all things from the very first, to write unto thee in order, most excellent Theophilus, 4. That thou also mightest know the certainty of those things, wherein thou hast been instructed."* Compare this to the "Gnostic New Age Bible" where "Gnosticism" says, "our real need is not forgiveness, but selfenlightenment."

This is exactly what Jesus said would happen in the last days before He returns. The Gnostics taught that Jesus can help us, but He is not needed for our salvation. This also Jesus said would happen in the last days, as in Matthew 24:5, *"For many shall come in my name, saying, I am Christ; and shall deceive many."* This is precisely what the New Age Movement teaches, embracing the Gnostic Gospel, which says 'I' am Christ. That we do not need Jesus to save us, we will save ourselves. These Gnostic gospels are therefore comfortable for the New Agers. They want change, and would like the possibility of uniting all the religions of the world, as was discussed in 1993 at the parliament of the World

Religions. The basic premise was, "Proselytizing should be forbidden, because trying to persuade others to believe in a particular religion, only raises the specter of exclusivity and the dreaded word – superiority." This of course is directly against our Christian faith, because it would, if enforced, be forbidden to spread the gospel of Jesus Christ all through the world, as Jesus told us to do.

Jesus also clearly mentions that this will happen in the last days, when we will have a world religion, as it says about the false prophet in Revelation 13:4, "... and they worshipped the beast (the anti-christ)... 5. And there was given unto him a mouth speaking great things and blasphemies... 6. And he opened his mouth in blasphemy against God... 8. And all that dwell upon the earth shall worship him (the anti-christ)." However, when this happens, Jesus will have taken His believers to heaven, through the Rapture, as Jesus said in Revelation 3:10, "I will also keep thee from the hour of temptation, which shall come upon all the world, to try them that dwell upon the earth." Does not Jesus clearly say here that His believers will not have to go through the terrible 7 year tribulation, but instead will be raptured?

Chapter 15

"And His feet shall stand in that day upon the Mount of Olives, which is before Jerusalem on the east..." Zechariah 14:4

—Ⓜ—

In Zechariah 12:8 it says, *"In that day shall the Lord defend the inhabitants of Jerusalem."* Also in Zechariah 14:3, *"Then shall the Lord go forth, and fight against those nations, as when He fought in the day of battle."* Here, at the end of the battle of Armageddon, is when the Lord returns, to fight against all the nations that have come up against Israel, and He will stand on the mount of Olives, which is just east of Jerusalem, *"and the mount of Olives shall cleave in the midst thereof towards the east and towards the west, and there shall be a very great valley; and half of the mountain shall remove toward the north, and half of it toward the south. 5. And ye shall flee to the valley of the mountains; for the valley of the mountains shall reach unto Azal: yea, ye shall flee, like as ye fled from before the earthquake in the days of Uzziah king of Judah: and the Lord my God shall come, and all the saints with thee."* Zechariah 14: 3-4

The apostle Luke also speaks about Jesus' return in Acts 1:6, *"When they therefore were come together* (on the Mount of Olives), *they asked of him, saying, Lord, wilt thou at this time restore again the kingdom to Israel?"* It is clear from this passage of scripture that the disciples understood that at one time Jesus would again restore the kingdom of Israel. However, Luke records Jesus' reply in Acts 1:7, *"... It is not for you to know the times or the seasons... 8. But ye shall receive power ... and ye shall be witnesses unto me, both in Jerusalem ... and unto the uttermost part of the earth. 9. And when he had spoken these things, while they beheld, he was taken up; and a cloud received him out of their sight. 10. And while they looked steadfastly toward heaven as he went up, behold, two men stood by them in white apparel; 11. Which also said, Ye men of Galilee, why stand ye gazing up into heaven? This same Jesus which is taken up from you into heaven, shall so come in like manner as ye have seen him go into heaven. 12. Then returned they unto Jerusalem from the mount called Olivet, which is from Jerusalem a sabbath day's journey."* Luke makes it very clear here, that Jesus will return to the Mount of Olives, the same as he left the Mount of Olives.

Since the angels said He would return "in like manner" as he ascended, He will return with the same Glorified body. Luke points out in chapter 24:39, *"Behold, my hands and my feet, that it is I myself: handle me, and see; for a spirit hath not flesh and bones, as ye see me have."* The apostle Jude also says that Jesus will return with the saints as in Jude 1:14, *"And Enoch also, the seventh from Adam, prophesied of these saying, behold, the Lord cometh, with ten thousands of his saints."* Already over 6000 years ago, Enoch, the seventh generation from Adam, prophesied that Jesus would return, with tens of thousands of His saints, just as in Zechariah 14:4 and Acts 1:11. Does this not tell the Amillennialist something about "the Bible is not a book foretelling the future" as many of them say? Here in Jude 1:14 Enoch already foretold over 6000 years ago that Jesus would return, with his saints, to earth.

Malachi, in chapter 3, foretold the future regarding Jesus' return as well. *"Behold, I will send my messenger, and he shall prepare the way before me: and the Lord, whom ye seek, shall suddenly come to His temple, even the messenger of the covenant, whom ye delight in: behold, He shall come, saith the Lord of hosts."* The temple Malachi refers to here has yet to be rebuilt before Jesus returns as in 2 Thess. 2:4, *"Who opposeth and exalteth above all that is called God, or that is worshipped; so that he* (the anti-christ) *as God sitteth in the temple of God, showing himself that he* (the anti-christ) *is God."* Malachi continues in 3:2, *"But who may abide the day of His coming? And who shall stand when He appeareth? For He is like refiner's fire, and like fuller's soap."* Micah also foretold that Jesus would return, and rule Israel on the new earth as in Micah 5:2, *"But thou, Bethlehem Ephratah, though thou be little among the thousands of Judah, yet out of thee shall He come forth unto me that is to be the 'ruler' in Israel; whose goings forth have been from of old, from everlasting."* Micah already said, that when Jesus returns, He will rule Israel during the Millennium, as we will see in the next chapter.

Chapter 16

"... and they lived and reigned with Christ a thousand years." Revelation 20:4

—⁊⁊⁊—

R evelation 20:4-6, *"And I saw thrones, and they that sat upon them, and judgment was given unto them, and I saw the souls of them that were beheaded for the witness of Jesus, and for the word of God, which had not worshipped the beast* (the anti-christ) *neither his image, neither had received his mark upon their foreheads, or in their hands; and they lived and reigned with Christ a thousand years. 5. But the rest of the dead lived not again until the thousand years were finished. This is the first resurrection. 6. Blessed and Holy is he that hath part in the first resurrection: on such the second death has no power, but they shall be priests of God and of Christ, and shall reign with Him a thousand years."* In Revelation 22: verses 2 and 3 we read of the Devil and Satan being bound for "a thousand years" after Jesus' return. That he would be cast into the bottomless pit "until the thousand years should be fulfilled" and then loosed again for a short time. When we read that we will live and reign with Christ for a thousand years spelled out so clearly in the Bible, there should be no doubt that this should be taken literally. Jesus Himself says in Revelation 1:1 *"The Revelation of Jesus Christ... 2. ... and of the testimony of*

Jesus Christ... 3. Blessed is he that readeth, and they that hear the words of this prophecy, and keep those things which are written therein..."

Yet the Amillennialist does not take Revelation 20:4 literally as Reverend Hoekema says in CRC Viewpoint, "Amillennialist believe that Christ's Second Coming will be amillennial – that is neither following, nor preceding an earthly golden age or an earthly millennial reign. We Amillennialist teach that the thousand year reign of Revelation 20:4-6 is not an earthly reign at all, but a reign of deceased believers with Christ in heaven. And we have come to this position on the basis of our interpretation of the book of Revelation."

But why? The book of Revelation clearly says in 20:4 "and they lived and reigned with Christ a thousand years," and in 1:1, "The Revelation of Jesus Christ." How can we refuse to take Him at His Word and not believe it? In 2 Peter 1:20 it says, *"Knowing this first, that no prophecy of the scripture is of private interpretation."* How then can we simply say, "that the thousand year reign of Revelation 20:4, is not an earthly reign at all", when Peter says clearly that no prophecy is of private interpretation, as the Amillennialist obviously do. Rev, Hoekema continues with, "Amillennialist do not understand the 'thousand years' in a strictly literal since. The Book of Revelation is full of symbolic numbers, and the thousand in the passage we're dealing with is one of these. Remember, that in the Bible, the number ten signifies completeness. Since a thousand is ten to the third power (10x10x10) we interpret the expression 'a thousand years' to mean a very long period of time. This period of time extends from the first coming of Christ (the beginning of Satan's defeat John 12:31-32) to just before Christ's Second Coming. This period ends with Christ's return since chapter 20 ends with the final judgment."

The Amillennialist are here making their own "private interpretation." Jesus did not say repeatedly in Revelation 20:

verses 2, 3, 4, 5, 6, and 7 "a very long period of time." Rather He says over and over, very specifically, "<u>a thousand years</u>."

Rev. Hoekema continues with, "How do Amillennialist interpret the words 'they came to life and reigned with Christ a thousand years (Rev 20:4)'? First of all, Amillennialist do not believe that these words refer to an earthly reign. There is no reference to the earth (or, for that matter, to Palestine or the Jews) in verses 4-6".

There is, however, a reference to the earth in Rev, 20: 7 and 8, *"And when the thousand years are expired, Satan shall be loosed out of his prison, 8. And shall go out to deceive the nations which are in the four quarters of the <u>earth</u>..."* It clearly says in Revelation 20:3, *"that he (Satan) shall go out to deceive the nations no more, until the thousand years be fulfilled."* Obviously, this refers to the same nations which are in the *"four corners of the <u>earth</u>."* that Satan goes out to deceive after the thousand years is fulfilled.

As for Hoekema saying there is no reference to the Jews or Palestine; we have already discussed in previous chapters that the Jews returned to their homeland, and how the Bible tells us that Jesus Christ will return to the Mount of Olives, and go into the temple in Jerusalem, from where He will rule over His people, Israel. Revelation 21 talks about the new city of Jerusalem that descends from heaven to earth. In verse 24 it says, *"And the nations of them which are saved shall walk in the light of it: and the kings of the <u>earth</u> do bring their glory and honour into it."*

Rev. Hoekema goes on to say, "Secondly, Amillennialist do not believe that 'came to life' means a physical resurrection... We, in fact, deny that this word describes a physical resurrection here." Revelation 20:4 lists the believers who were killed because they refused to worship the beast or take his mark. At the end of the verse it says, *"they lived and reigned with Christ a thousand years."* Then in verse 5 it says, *"... This is the first resurrection."* Is this unclear? I cannot imagine anyone twisting this to mean something else. Do they think God writes one thing while meaning something else, just to trick us?

1 John 3:2 says, *"Beloved, now are we the sons of God, and it doth not appear what we shall be: but we know that when he shall appear, we shall be like him; for we shall se him as he is."* Phillipians 3:21, *"Who (Jesus Christ) shall change our vile body, that it may be fashioned like unto his glorious body..."*

Revelation tells us more about those people who were killed and then resurrected to live and reign with Christ a thousand years. Revelation 6:9-11, *"... I saw under the altar the souls of those that were slain for the word of God, and for the testimony which they held: ... 11. And white robes were given unto every one of them; and it was said unto them, that they should rest yet for a little season, until their fellowservants also and their bretheren, that should be killed as they were, should be fulfilled."* Revelation 7:13-16, *"... What are these which are arrayed in white robes? And whence came they? 14... These are they which came out of <u>great tribulation</u>, and have washed their robes, and made them white in the blood of the Lamb. Therefore they are before the throne of God, and serve him day and night in his <u>temple</u>: and he that sitteth on the throne shall dwell among them. 16. They shall hunger no more; neither thirst any more..."* This is a physical resurrection. They are the believers who were killed during the "great tribulation" and will live and reign with Christ in the new temple in Jerusalem for a thousand years.

Isaiah 65:17, *"For, behold, I create new heavens and a new earth: and the former shall not be remembered, nor come into mind. 18. But be ye glad and rejoice for ever in that which I create: for, behold, I create Jerusalem a rejoicing, and her people a joy. 19. And I will rejoice in Jerusalem and joy in my people; and the voice of weeping shall no more be heard in her, nor the voice of crying. 20.*

There shall no more thence be an infant of days, nor an old man that hath not filled his days; for the child shall die an hundred years old, but the sinner being an hundred years old shall be accursed." We see here from Isaiah 65: 17-20, that there will be sinners on this new earth, where also, the wolf will feed with the lamb during this same period of time. This period of time could not be on this present day earth, because the wolf and the lamb do not normally feed together here on this earth today. Also, this passage from Isaiah could not describe heaven because we know that there will be no sinners in heaven. It could also not describe the final new earth, when the 1000 year Millennium is over as described in Revelation 21: 1, *"And I saw a new heaven and a new earth for the first heaven and the first earth were passed away; and there was no more sea. 2. And I John saw the Holy city new Jerusalem, coming down from God out of heaven, prepared as a bride adorned for her husband. 3. And I heard a great voice out of heaven saying, behold, God is with men, and He will dwell with them ... and God himself shall be with them, and be their God. 4. And God shall wipe away all tears from their eyes, and there shall be no more death, neither sorrow, nor crying, neither shall there be any more pain."*

So what is this period of time Isaiah is referring to, where there are still sinners on a new earth, and where the wolf and the lamb feed together? Since it cannot be this present earthly situation, nor could it be heaven, nor could it be the new earth after the 1000 year Millennium, we can only conclude that Isaiah 65:17-20 is talking about the 1000 year Millennium. And Isaiah says that during this time, there will be no weeping, but joy in God's people, yet the sinner being 100 years old, will be accursed. This is a most assured indication of scripture that there will indeed be a 1000 year Millennium, where Christ will reign on earth. The same thousand year period that Revelation 20 speaks about. It is all so easy to understand the scriptures when one reads them

literally, instead of trying to make all kinds of different interpretations that are not really said in the Bible.

All Amillennialist believe there will be no 1000 year
millennium, as Rev. Verbrugge says, "The millennium is not
a 1000 years. Christ will reign from His ascension till He
returns. That is the Millennium, the so-called 1000 years.
The so-called 1000 years are symbolic. We are called to
reign over this earth right now, right here. The kingdom of
this world has become the kingdom of God, no matter how
messed up it is in the world." Verbrugge also says, "When
Jesus walked on earth, He brought the kingdom of God here
on earth. Therefore the kingdom of God has already come
here on earth now. We live and reign with Christ now."

My response would be, that the so-called 1000 years, as
Verbrugge says, are indeed called "a thousand years" repeatedly in the Bible as we have discussed previously. Since
Revelation 1:1 says, *"The Revelation of Jesus Christ"*, how
can anyone so boldly doubt His words when He says in
Revelation 20:4, *"And they lived and reigned with Christ a
thousand years"*, and refer to that as "so-called 1000 years"?

The Bible does not say that we live and reign with Christ
now. The time described that we will live and reign with
Christ is not until after the rapture, which is followed by the
seven year tribulation period with the four horsemen, and the
anti-christ, and Armageddon. Revelation 20:4 says, *"And I
saw thrones, and they that sat upon them, and judgment was
given unto them."* This has not happened yet. The events
and judgments predicted in Revelation have yet to happen
in a chronological order before Christ returns. Therefore,
we could not already be reigning with Him as Verbrugge
says. Why is it that Amillennialist do not want to read the
Bible literally? This causes all kinds of misinterpretations.
Verbrugge also says, "The kingdom of God has already
come here on earth now." Jesus Christ taught us to pray,
"Our Father, Who art in heaven, Thy kingdom come, Thy

will be done, on earth, as it is in heaven ..." Why would we need to pray this if we were already reigning with Him in His kingdom here on earth? Clearly, the coming of God's kingdom has not yet happened, and the fact that this is the very first petition of the Lord's Prayer, should tell us how important the coming of His kingdom should be for us! *"... Even so, come, Lord Jesus."* Revelation 22:20

When Christ comes to establish His kingdom on earth, he will descend to earth to the Mount of Olives as in Zechariah 14:4, and will enter Jerusalem through the Eastern Gate. Ezekiel 44:1 says, *"Then he brought me back the way of the gate of the outward sanctuary which looketh toward the east; and it was shut. 2. Then said the Lord unto me, this gate shall be shut, it shall not be opened, and no man shall enter in by it; because the Lord, the God of Israel, hath entered in by it, therefore it shall be shut. 3. It is for the prince (Jesus); the prince, he shall sit in it to eat bread before the Lord; He shall enter by the way of the porch of that gate, and shall go out by the way of the same."* Ezekiel says here, that Jesus (after He returns to earth on the Mount of Olives), will again enter Jerusalem through the Eastern Gate (which looks toward the east), as He did when He entered Jerusalem for the first time on Palm Sunday – just before He was to be crucified. This is the same gate, of which the Lord said in Ezekiel 44:1-2, *"It shall be shut, it shall not be opened, ... 3... till the prince* (Jesus) *enter in by it."* The Eastern Gate has indeed been walled shut, as the Lord promised it would be in Ezekiel, and has been to this day. It will stay shut until Jesus returns again to the Mount of Olives, to set up His kingdom on the new earth during the 1000 year Millennium.

Contrary to this, the Amillennialist view is that God's kingdom is already present in the world now, as Rev Hoekema says in CRC Viewpoint, "Amillennialist hold that the kingdom of God is now present in the world as the victorious Christ is ruling His people by his Word and Spirit."

"We Have Also A More Sure Word Of Prophecy 2 Peter 1:19However, this is not what the Bible says, that He is King over the earth now. Zechariah 44:4 says, *"And His feet shall stand in that day* (the day after the Lord fought against all the nations that came up to do battle against Jerusalem, as in Zech. 14:1-2) *upon the Mount of Olives, ... 9. And the Lord shall be king over all the earth: in that day shall there be one Lord, and His name one."* Here we see that Jesus will not be king and ruler over the earth, until He returns on the Mount of Olives. And we know that has not happened yet. That will not happen until after the seven year tribulation, with the anti-christ, the four horsemen, and Armageddon, has finished, and all the nations have come up against Jerusalem to do battle. None of these has happened yet, although they seem to be very close, if one watches what is happening in the world today.

Why can the Amillennialist not read the Bible literally? This is the reason that Rev. Bultema was "deposed." He defended the dispensationalist position, which is to take the Bible literally, as was professor D. H. Kromminga, who believed in a future Millennium, as Rev. Hoekema says in CRC Viewpoint. He also says on page 31, "These Old Testament prophecies don't point to a thousand year period before the end." Actually, however, the Old Testament prophesies do indeed point to a thousand year period on the new earth, where the wolf will feed with the lamb, while there is still sin on this new earth at the same time, as in Isaiah 60:18, *"Violence shall no more be heard in thy land, wasting nor destruction within thy borders; but thou shalt call thy walls salvation, and thy gates Praise. 19. The sun shall be no more thy light by day, neither for brightness shall the moon give light unto thee; but the Lord shall be unto thee an everlasting light, and thy God thy glory. 20. The sun shall no more go down; neither shall the moon withdraw itself: for the Lord shall be thine everlasting light, and the days of thy mourning shall be ended. 21. Thy people shall also be all righteous:*

they shall inherit the land forever..." Isaiah says here how good it will be on the new earth. In verse 12, though, he says, *"For the nation and kingdom that will not serve Thee shall perish: yea, those nations shall be utterly wasted."* Verses 18-21 show us how beautiful it will be on the new earth; verse 12 tells us that there will still be some sin and war at the same time. This period of time could not be the present earth, since the wolf and the lamb do not feed together yet on this earth, while this period of time could also not point to heaven, since there will be no sin in heaven, as the scriptures tell us. Therefore the only explanation for this period of time is that it is indeed the 1000 year Millennium, as so clearly described in Revelation 20:4-6.

Isaiah 65 also points to a 1000 year Millennium in verse 17. Isaiah says, *"For, behold, I create new heavens and a new earth: and the former shall not be remembered, nor come into mind. 18. But be ye glad and rejoice forever in that which I create: for, behold, I create Jerusalem a rejoicing, and her people a joy. 19. And I will rejoice in Jerusalem, and joy in my people, and the voice of weeping shall no more be heard in her, nor the voice of crying."* Here again, Isaiah clearly shows how good it will be on the new earth, while the next verse, 20, says, *"There shall be no more thence an infant of days, nor an old man that hath not filled his days: for the child shall die an hundred years old; but the sinner being an hundred years old shall be accursed."*

Here again, we see there will be sinners on this new earth, and death. Yet verse 25 says, *"The wolf and the lamb shall feed together, and the lion shall eat straw like the bullock."* Obviously, this is not referring to this present day earth. This is not until Jesus returns. It is therefore again clear that this period mentioned must be the 1000 year Millennium, and it is mentioned by many more prophets in the Old Testament.

Rev. Hoekema says in CRC Viewpoint, "We look next at 1 Thessalonians 3:13, 'May He (the Lord) strengthen your hearts, so that you will be blameless and holy in the presence of our God and Father, when our Lord Jesus comes with all His holy ones (or saints).' not just with some of them. How does this leave room for other saints born after Christ's Second Coming and converted during the Millennium?"

We read in Revelation 6:15-7:1, *"And the kings of the earth, and the great men, and the rich men, and the chief captains, and the mighty men, and the bondmen, and every free man, hid themselves in the dens and in the rocks of the mountains; 16. And said to the mountains and rocks, Fall on us, and hide us from the face of him that sitteth on the throne, and from the wrath of the lamb: 17. For the great day of his wrath has come; who shall be able to stand? 7:1. And after these things I saw four angels standing on the four corners of the earth ... 3. Saying, hurt not the earth, neither the sea, nor the trees, till we have sealed the servants of our God in their foreheads. 4. And I heard the number of them which were sealed: and there were sealed an hundred and forty and four thousand of all the tribes of the children of Israel. 5. Of the tribe of Judah were sealed twelve thousand ..."* etc.

The apostle John here in Revelation 7, tells us that 144,000 Jews will be sealed to witness during the tribulation time, after the believers in Jesus Christ have already been raptured. The anti-christ cannot hurt those who have been sealed during this terrible tribulation time, but these Jews will be witnesses to the world to share the gospel of Jesus Christ. This answers Rev. Hoekema's question about Jesus returning with all his saints. When Jesus raptured His believers before the seven year tribulation period, the people left behind have one more chance to believe in Jesus Christ through the 144,000 Jews, who became followers and witnesses of Christ, after the rapture. Quite simply, all the saints in heaven come back with Christ when He does. That does not say there cannot be any more added who have been converted during the tribulation period, for indeed,

Revelation 20:4 lists them, and they are added at the end of the seven year tribulation after Jesus has returned.

Revelation 14:1 says, *"And I looked, and, lo, a Lamb stood on the mount Zion, and with him an hundred and forty and four thousand, having his Father's name written in their foreheads."* And in verse 3, *"...and no man could learn that song but the hundred and forty and four thousand, which were redeemed from the earth."* These passages from Revelation 7 and 14 are most likely not in agreement with the Amillennialist, especially with Rev. Vander Waal, who says on page 135, "Revelation 17 and 18 are not talking about a heathen city or an empire; they are talking about Israel, the covenant people who killed the prophets." And on page 139, "Jesus shows us how the Lord finally dismisses Jerusalem, the city that slaughtered the Lamb. Henceforth He will no longer recognize the Jews as His People."

Not only did the Lord not dismiss His chosen people, He brought them back to their homeland again, and He will also use them to be His witnesses during the 7 year tribulation period (which could start at any moment, if we read the signs correctly of all that is happening in the world today). Rev, Hoekema says in CRC Viewpoint, "We are not to expect that people will be saved after Christ's return. Let's examine the relevant scripture passages. First look again at Matthew 24:31, 'And he (the Son of man coming in the clouds) will send his angels with a loud trumpet call, and they will gather his elect from the four winds, from one end of the heavens to the other.' Dispensationalist commonly interpreted this passage as referring only to the gathering of the Jewish elect at the end of the tribulation period ... what room is left for the gathering of still more elect after Christ's Second Coming? ... How does this leave room for other saints born after Christ's Second Coming and converted during the millennium?"

We have already discussed the believers converted during the tribulation period who are listed in Revelation

20:4, *"... and I saw the souls of them that were beheaded for the witness of Jesus, and for the Word of God, and which had not worshipped the beast, neither his image, neither had received his mark..."* And we discussed the 144,000 witnesses, the sealed Jews who now believe in Jesus Christ and are scattered around the earth. They will be largely responsible for converting many of the people of Israel, referred to in Revelation 12:13-17 as, "the woman which brought forth the man child" and "the remnant of her seed, which keep the commandments of God and the testimony of Jesus Christ." (the Jews)

As far as gathering during the tribulation period, let us have a look at Revelation 11:1-3, *"And there was given me a reed like unto a rod: and the angel stood, saying, Rise, and measure the temple of God, and the altar, and them that worship therein. 2. But the court which is without the temple, leave out, and measure it not; for it is given unto the gentiles: and the holy city shall they tread under foot forty and two months. 3 And I will give power unto my two witnesses, and they shall prophesy a thousand two hundred and three-score days, clothed in sackcloth."* Revelation says here, that the gentiles will tread Jerusalem under foot for 3½ years, and then the two witnesses will get power to prophesy for another 3½ years, being the second half of the 7 year tribulation period, as mentioned in Daniel 9:27, *"And he* (the anti-christ) *shall confirm the covenant with many for one week* (7 years) *and in the midst of the week, he* (the anti-christ) *shall cause the sacrifice and the oblation to cease"* and, as in 2 Thessalonians 2:4, he sets himself up in the temple as god.

Daniel also refers to these 3½ years in Dan. 12:6, *"...how long shall it be to the end of these wonders? 7. And I heard the man clothed in linen, ... that it shall be for a time,* (1 year) *times,* (2 years) *and a half a time (1/2 a year)"* – again, 3½ years of tribulation. Similarly, in Revelation 12:12, *" Woe to the inhabitants of the earth and the sea, for the devil is come down unto you, having great wrath, because he knoweth that he hath but as short time. 13. And when the dragon* (Satan) *saw that he was cast to the earth, he persecuted the woman which brought forth the man child* (Jesus Christ). *14. And to the woman* (Israel) *were given two wings of a great eagle, that she might fly into the wilderness, into her place, where she is nourished for a time, and times, and half a time, from the face of the serpent."* – again referring to the last 3½ years of the tribulation. Here we see that Satan will be cast down to the earth for the last 3½ years of the tribulation, and the Jewish believers will be protected by God and nourished by Him for that time. Verse 10 says, *"And I heard a loud voice saying in heaven, Now is come salvation, and strength, and the kingdom of our God, and the power of his Christ:"* This shows that Satan is cast to the earth just before Jesus returns, and not, like the Amillennialist and Rev Hoekema in CRC Viewpoint says, at the time of Christ's earthly ministry.

In all these passages of scripture, it is clear that God's word says that there will be a terrible tribulation, when Satan has come down to earth, just as Jesus said in Matthew 24:21, *"For then* (during the last 3 ½ years of the tribulation) *shall be great tribulation, such as was not from the beginning of the world to this time, no, nor ever shall be."* Surely no period of history could be singled out as being so much worse than any other in earth's history as to be compared to this "great tribulation." It hasn't happened yet! Furthermore, in verse 29, *"Immediately after the tribulation of those days shall the sun be darkened, and the moon shall not give her light, and the stars shall fall from heaven, and the powers of heaven shall be shaken:"* News Flash – that hasn't happened yet either! Finally, Matthew 24:30, *"And then shall appear the sign of the Son of man in heaven... and they shall see the Son of man coming in the clouds of heaven with power and great glory."*

This makes it absolutely certain that Matthew 24:21 is referring to the final "great" tribulation followed by Jesus return. Yet Rev. Verbrugge says, "The dispensationalist view of the rapture and the 7 year tribulation stirs up the imagination. It does not hold up the creationist view of the church." I would like to hear how he then would interpret Matthew 24:21, in light of all we have just discussed, and explain how that does not hold up to the creationist view of the church.

Rev. Vander Waal also has a totally different interpretation of the "last time" prophecies. He says on page 67, "To get a better grasp of Hal Lindsay's views on the last things, bear in mind the following four theses he defends.

(1.) Christ's return will not occur at the same time as the rapture, the day the believers are taken up to heaven.

(2.) After the rapture there will be a 7 year period during which people will still be able to repent and turn to Christ.

(3.) During that 7 year period, many of the biblical prophecies will be fulfilled.

(4.) The Jews will play a major role in the 7 year period." He also says, "These four points cannot be defended on Scriptural grounds. Let's look at them one by one.

(1.) According to 1 Thessalonians 4, the believers will be taken up to meet Christ as He returns, thus we may not separate the 'Rapture' from Christ's return.

(2.) There is no seven year period following the rapture. The idea of such a period is based on an arbitrary reading of Revelation 11:2-3. Moreover, Scripture says nothing about any opportunity for repentance and conversion after Christ's return.

(3.) It's typical of sectarian thinking that all sorts of prophecies are supposed to be fulfilled during the seven year period. Sectarians seek a temporal framework within which they can place sensational events. This means that a special period must be created. They don't seem to realize that those

Old Testament prophesies they hope to see fulfilled in the seven year period, have already been fulfilled.

(4.) The claim that we now live in the age of the church and that there will be another, in which the Jews play a dominant role, is completely in conflict with the function the Lord has assigned to the church, as the body of believers. The special period is created to make room for the realization of age-old Jewish dreams.

Thus, Hal Lindsay's vision of the last things is to be rejected. It is in conflict with the confession of the Reformation, which does not teach that the Jewish people and the city of Jerusalem will be dominant at the end of time. Lindsay's thoughts represent a form of eschatologized Judaism."

It appears that Rev. Vander Waal bases his information on religious doctrine, rather than the Holy Bible. My comment for his first point is that we have dealt with this in detail in chapter 3. The Rapture. This is not the time of Christ's return, but rather, He meets his bride in the air, to keep his followers from the *"hour of temptation that shall come upon all the world, to try them that dwell upon the earth"* Revelation 3:10. He takes them back with Him to Heaven.

Skipping to point # 3, we have clearly seen in previous chapters, that the 7 year tribulation, as mentioned by Jesus in Matthew 24:21, and referred to as well in Revelation and Daniel, has not yet been fulfilled, contrary to what Vander Waal says.

Regarding point #4, again contrary to what Vander Waal says, the Jews, and the city of Jerusalem will be dominant at the end time, as we have clearly seen from scripture. In fact, the number of references in the Bible to the city of Jerusalem, and the temple, and the Jewish witnesses, and the Jewish people fleeing from anti-christ, all just preceding Christ's return, are overwhelming.

As for point #2, Vander Waal says, "Moreover, scripture says nothing about any opportunity for repentance and conversion after Christ's return." We have just read in Revelation 11:1-3 about the two witnesses who will prophesy during the last 3½ years of the tribulation, to bring the gospel to the people who are left behind after the rapture, not to mention the 144,000 sealed witnesses and all the people they will convert. Revelation also tells us about all those believers who refused the mark of the anti-christ. I believe this answers his second point.

Continuing with Revelation 11:4, *"These* (the two witnesses) *are the two olive trees ... 5. And if any man will hurt them, fire proceedeth out of their mouth and devoureth their enemies ... 6. These have power to shut heaven ... 7. And when they shall have finished their testimony, the beast* (the anti-christ), *that ascendeth out of the bottomless pit shall make war against them* (the two witnesses), *and shall overcome them, and kill them. 8 And their dead bodies shall lie in the street of the great city* (Jerusalem), *which spiritually is called Sodom and Egypt, where also our Lord was crucified. 9. And they of the people and kindreds and tongues and nations shall see their dead bodies three days and a half, and shall not suffer their dead bodies to be put in graves. 10. And they that dwell upon the earth shall rejoice over them, and make merry, and shall send gifts one to another; because the two prophets tormented them that dwelt on the earth. 11. And after three and a half days, the spirit of life from God entered into them, and they stood upon their feet; and great fear fell upon them which saw them."*

Verse 9 says that the whole earth could see their dead bodies lie in the streets of Jerusalem, something that has not even been possible until today with satellite TV, and computers, etc. Technology, for the first time in history, makes it possible to see everything that is happening anywhere in the world, and lets the entire world watch it "live". This, finally, makes it possible for this prophecy, made 2000 years ago, to be literally fulfilled.

Verses 8-10 show how wicked the people will get during the tribulation period, until verse 11, when the Lord miraculously brings the two witnesses back to life, and great fear falls upon the ungodly people. The comparisons to "Sodom and Egypt" reveal a society as corrupt and wicked as two of the worst in history. Sodom, when God himself destroyed them for their evil ways, and Egypt, when God dealt with them by sending the terrible plagues. Yet, in spite of this clear indication of the wickedness in the world during this time of the 7 year tribulation, the Amillennialist still will not believe that Matthew 24:21 points to the "end time" just before Jesus returns.

Hoekema says in CRC Viewpoint, "Amillennialist believe that the return of Christ will be preceded by certain signs: the preaching of the gospel to all nations, the great tribulation, the great apostasy or rebellion, and the coming of a personal anti-christ. But we do not believe that these events will take place only in the time before Christ's return. For they have been present in some sense from the very beginning of the Christian era, and are present now."

How can he say, "have been present from the very beginning of the Christian era", when Christ says in Matthew 24:21, *"For then shall be great tribulation such as was not since the beginning of the world to this time, no, nor ever shall be."*

We know that it points to the "end time" because the next verse says, *"Immediately after the tribulation of those days,* (the days of the end time) *shall the sun be darkened ... and they shall see the Son of man coming on the clouds of heaven with power and great glory."* How can we not interpret this literally as God's word?

I am glad however, that Rev. Hoekema, contrary to Rev. Vander Waal and Rev. Verbrugge at least, says, "Amillennialist believe that the return of Christ will be preceded by ... the great tribulation, the great apostasy or rebellion, and the coming of a personal anti-christ." This I can certainly agree with, as the apostle Peter says in 2 Peter 1:19, *"We have also a more sure word of prophecy ... 20. Knowing this first, that no prophecy of the scripture is of any private interpretation."* The apostle Paul also says in 2 Timothy 3:16, *"All scripture is given by inspiration of God, and is profitable for doctrine."*

Chapter 17

"The wolf also shall dwell with the lamb, and the leopard shall lie down with the kid." Isaiah 11:6

—ᴍ—

Zechariah 14:3, *"Then shall the Lord go forth, and fight against those nations, as when He fought in the day of battle. 4. And his feet shall stand in that day upon the mount of Olives, which is before Jerusalem on the East, and the mount of Olives shall cleave in the midst thereof toward the East and toward the west, and there shall be a very great valley; and half of the mountain shall remove toward the north, and half of it toward the south. 5. ... and the Lord my God shall come, and all the saints with thee. 6. And it shall come to pass in that day, that the light shall not be clear, nor dark: 7. But it shall be one day which shall be known to the Lord, not day, nor night: but it shall come to pass, that at evening time it shall be light. 8. And it shall be in that day, that living waters shall go out from Jerusalem; ... 9. And the Lord shall be king over all the earth: in that day shall there be one Lord, and His name one. ... 11. ... and there shall be no more utter destruction, but Jerusalem shall be safely inhabited."*

We see here, that the Lord will make an end to the battle of Armageddon in Zech. 14:3, and after that, verse 9 says, *"And the Lord shall be king over all the earth."* Also in

Isaiah 11, we read about the new earth, as in Isaiah 11:1, *"And there shall come forth a rod out of the stem of Jesse, and a Branch shall grow out of his roots: 2. And the spirit of the Lord shall rest upon Him, the spirit of wisdom and understanding, the spirit of counsel and might, the spirit of knowledge and of the fear of the Lord; 3. And shall make him of quick understanding in the fear of the Lord: ... 4. But with righteousness shall He judge the poor, and reprove with equity for the meek of the earth: and He shall smite the earth with the rod of His mouth, and with the breath of his lips shall He slay the wicked."* It is clear from verse 4 that the Lord will stop the wickedness that still seems to exist on the new earth, indicating that there is indeed a 1000 year millennium. From the following verses we see that Isaiah is talking here about the new earth, where Jesus rules, as in Isaiah 11:6, *"The wolf shall dwell with the lamb, and the leopard shall lie down with the kid; and the calf and young lion and the fatling together; and a little child shall lead them. 7. And the cow and the bear shall feed; their young ones shall lie down together: and the lion shall eat straw like the ox. 8. And the sucking child shall play on the hole of the asp, and the weaned child shall put his hand on the cockatrice' den. 9. They shall not hurt nor destroy in all my holy mountain: for the earth shall be full of the knowledge of the Lord, as the waters cover the sea."*

Isaiah describes in verses 6-9 the future millennial reign of Christ as a time in which the curse of sin and violence will be lifted from he earth. Animals will no longer kill to eat, and violence will be eliminated, as other old time prophesies have confirmed. (Ezekiel 34:25-28, Hosea 2:18.)

Isaiah 40:1, *"Comfort ye, comfort ye my people, saith your God. 2. Speak ye comfortably to Jerusalem, and cry unto her, that her warfare is accomplished, that her iniquity is pardoned: ... 5. And the glory of the Lamb shall be revealed, and all flesh shall see it together: for the mouth of the Lord hath spoken it."*

All through scripture the prophets mention the new earth, as in Isaiah 60:18, *"Violence shall no more be heard in thy land, wasting nor destruction within thy borders... 19. The sun shall be no more thy light by day, neither for brightness shall the moon give light unto thee: but the Lord shall be unto thee an everlasting light, and thy God thy glory... 21. Thy people also shall be all righteous: they shall inherit the land for ever..."*

In all these passages of scripture, we see that Jesus, will rule on the new earth with a rod of iron to keep the wicked under control, until the end of the 1000 year millennium. Then Satan will be loosed for a little season, and will deceive the nations once more, until he will be cast into the lake of fire forever.

Rev. Hoekema has this to say about the reign of Christ on the new earth, "Believers will enter into everlasting glory on the new earth. The concept of the new earth is so important, that we should give it more than a passing thought. Many Christians think they will spend eternity in some heaven far off in space ... but is our eternal home somewhere up in the air? Doesn't the Bible clearly teach that we will live in resurrection bodies on a new earth?" (Amen brother, I certainly agree with you here: see Isaiah 65:17, 2 Peter 3:13, Revelation 21:1). And what will this life be like? Hoekema continues, "The Old Testament tells us that God's people will possess the land of promise forever, that the wolf will live with the lamb, and that the earth will be as full of the knowledge of the Lord as the waters cover the sea." I can certainly agree wholeheartedly with Rev. Hoekema here, and I am glad that we have some interpretations in common.

Rev. Hoekema goes on to say, however, "These old testament prophecies don't point to a thousand-year period before the end. Rather they describe the life of God's people on the new earth for eternity." and I cannot be in agreement with him here. Yes, God's people will live on the new earth for eternity, as the prophets describe it. However, the same prophecies do point to a "thousand year" period as well. How else can we interpret Isaiah 65:20, *"There shall be no more thence an infant of days, nor an old man that hath not filled his days; for the child shall die an hundred years old, but the sinner being an hundred years old, shall be accursed."* Hoekema himself said, in reference to Isaiah 65:17, "we will live in resurrection bodies on a new earth." Verse 19 says, *"And I will rejoice in Jerusalem, and joy in my people: and the voice of weeping shall be no more heard in her, nor the voice of crying."* Yet in verse 20, we see that there is still sin on this new earth as well. This verse 20 is the strongest indication yet, that there will be a 1000 year millennium. This is the only period of time when the wolf and lamb can feed together and yet there are still sinners, as we have discussed previously. And, this can not happen when the final new earth and the new heaven will be established as in Revelation 21:1, *"And I saw a new heaven and a new earth: for the first heaven and the first earth were passed away... 3. ... Behold, the tabernacle of God is with men, and He will dwell with them, and they shall be His people, and God Himself shall be with them, and be their God. 4. And God shall wipe away all tears from their eyes, and there shall be no more death, neither sorrow, nor crying, neither shall there be any more pain: for the former things are passed away."* Rev. 21:1-5 shows, that Isaiah 65 could not also be talking about this same period of the final new heaven and the new earth, because here in Rev. 21:1-5, there is no more death, nor sin, while Isaiah 65:20 clearly says there is sin. Revelation 20 clearly shows that there will yet be war and death at the end of the 1000 year millennium, when Satan is loosed "out of his prison ... to deceive the nations", until he is cast into the lake of fire forever. At the end of the 1000 year millennium, begins the kingdom that Daniel speaks about in Daniel 2:44, *"And in the days of these kings shall the God of heaven set up a kingdom, which shall never be destroyed..."* This kingdom will therefore continue forever, after the 1000 year millennium, as God's word so clearly says.

But, remember, that before the 1000 year millennium will start, there will be the Rapture of the church, when Jesus will take His believers to heaven with Him. Then, on earth, the terrible 7 year tribulation period will begin, and as we see things unfolding on earth to-day, that might not be far away. At this very moment the European countries with the U.S. are in a dialogue with Iran to discuss the threat of their nuclear capability, which is a great concern, since the head of Iran's government said some time ago that Iran will not rest until Israel is wiped "off the map."

This is exactly what the Bible has foretold in Psalm 83:4, *"They have said, Come, and let us cut them off from being a nation; that the name of Israel may be no more in remembrance."* The fact that Russia has close ties with Iran as they threaten Israel, is also foretold in Ezekiel 38, *"... Gog, the land of Magog, the chief prince of Meshech and Tubal, ... Persia, Ethiopia, and Libya with them: ... 15. And thou shalt come from thy place out of the north parts, ... 16. And thou shalt come up against my people of Israel, as a cloud to cover the land; it shall be in the latter days,"*

Also, the war in Iraq gets more violent by the day, and could turn into a civil war at any time. There are so many civil wars at this moment, just as Jesus foretold in Matthew, 24:6, *"And ye shall hear of wars and rumors of wars."*

With the increased amount of suicide bombers everywhere, terrorist attacks are possible anywhere now, as we have just seen with the arrest of a large number of people connected with terrorist involvement in Brampton, Ontario (our home town from 1953), which indicates that no place on earth is immune from terrorist attack today. The amount of explosives found in this building was three times as much as was needed to blow up the large building in Oklahoma where 168 people died. If the large amount of explosives that was found in this building had been detonated at the time of the arrest, it could have leveled several city blocks.

We can expect more terrorist attacks like 9-11 and Madrid and London and Bali etc, as the Bible says in Daniel 12:1, *"... and there shall be a time of trouble, such as never was since there was a nation even to that same time: and at that time thy people shall be delivered,"* just as Jesus says in Matthew 24:21, *"For then shall be great tribulation, such as was not since the beginning of the world, to this time, no, nor ever shall be."* As we see how all the other signs mentioned by Jesus in Matthew 24 are happening around us, like the bird flu spreading from human to human now, and aids is spreading out of control, as is the war on drugs, and I'm reminded that Jesus said in Matthew 24:37, *"But as the days of Noah were, so shall also the coming of the Son of man be."* And in verse 31 Jesus makes it clear that, *"... when ye see these things come to pass, know ye that the kingdom of God is nigh at hand."*

Revelation 20:6 says, *"Blessed and Holy is he that hath part in the first resurrection: on such the second death hath no power, but they shall be priests of God and of Christ, and shall reign with Him a thousand years."*

Daniel 2:44, *"And in the days of these kings shall the God of heaven set up a kingdom which shall never be destroyed."*

Isaiah 65:17, *"For, Behold, I create 'new heavens and a new earth': and the former shall not be remembered, nor come into mind. 18. But be ye glad and rejoice for ever in that which I create: for, behold, I create Jerusalem a rejoicing, and her people a joy. 19. And I will rejoice in Jerusalem, and joy in my people: and the voice of weeping shall be no more heard in her, nor the voice of crying."*

Isaiah 35:5, *"Then the eyes of the blind shall be opened, and the ears of the deaf shall be unstopped. 6. Then shall the lame man leap as an hart, and the tongue of the dumb sing: for in the wilderness shall waters break out, and streams in the desert."*

Isaiah 65:21, *"And they shall build houses, and inhabit them; and they shall plant vineyards and eat the fruit of them. 22. They shall not build and another inhabit; they shall not plant and another eat: for as the days of a tree are the days of my people, and mine elect shall long enjoy the works of their hands. 23. They shall not labour in vain, nor bring forth for trouble; for they are the seed of the blessed of the Lord, and their offspring with them. 24. And it shall come to pass, that before they call, I will answer; and while they are yet speaking I will hear."*

Epilogue

—ww—

I sincerely hope that the reading of this book has been a blessing to you. If we believe that Jesus died for our sins on the cross, we can also know that He will return for us soon with the rapture. He said in Luke 21:31, *"... when you see 'these things' come to pass, know ye that the kingdom of God is nigh at hand."* Many of "these things" are already happening today. These are the signs that He will be coming soon, to "gather His elect."

However, if you are not sure that you belong with the believers that will be taken up by Jesus when He returns, remember that Jesus died on the cross for all of our sins, every one of us. If we believe in Him, and ask Him to come into our heart, we still have some time left to get to know Him as our personal savior. The Bible says, *"That if thou shalt confess with thy mouth the Lord Jesus, and believe in thine heart that God raised him from the dead, thou shalt be saved."* Romans 11:9

In Acts 16:30 the keeper of the prison asked the Apostle Paul and his friend Silas, *"Sirs, what must I do to be saved?" 31. And they said, Believe on the Lord Jesus Christ and thou shalt be saved, and thy house."*

John 3:16, *"For God so loved the world, that he gave his only begotten Son, that whosoever believeth in him should not perish, but have everlasting life."*

As God's children, we will not have to go through the terrible tribulation time on earth, which Jesus spoke of in Matthew 24:21, *"For 'then' shall be great tribulation, such as was not since the beginning of the world to this time, no, nor ever shall be."* This will be the time, when the antichrist will be revealed for the first time to the world and he will rule the whole earth with his power, and start the 'mark of the beast' — 666. It will also be a time of God's wrath upon the earth.

Instead we will go to heaven with Jesus. Then we will return with Him, after the 7 tribulation years are finished, when Jesus will set His feet again on the Mount of Olives to begin His 1000 year millennium kingdom on the new earth, as in Revelation 20:4, *"And they lived and reigned with Christ a thousand years."*

And when the thousand years are finished, we will reign with Christ forever on the new earth, as in Revelation 21:1-7, *"Where there shall no more be death, neither sorrow, nor crying, neither shall there be any more pain, for the former things are passed away."*

If we believe therefore, that Jesus is our personal savior, who died on the cross for our sins, this will be our beautiful future with Jesus. Revelation 21:1-7, *"God is with men, and He will dwell with men, and they shall be His people, and God Himself shall be with them, and be their God."*

If you want to know more about God's love for us, and His amazing grace through Bible prophecy, tune in to the Jack Van Impe Ministry. He has a weekly TV or radio presentation in every country of the world.

As a partner of faith with the Van Impe ministries, I sincerely hope that you will get a blessing, as my wife and I do, from Jack Van Impe's interpretation of God's prophetic word.

"... We shall not all sleep, but we shall all be changed. In a moment, in the twinkling of an eye, at the last trump: for the trumpet shall sound, and the dead shall be raised incorruptible, and we shall be changed."   1 Corinthians 15:51-52

"For the Lord himself shall descend from heaven with a shout, with the voice of the archangel, and with the trump of God: and the dead in Christ shall rise first: Then we which are alive and remain shall be caught up together with them in the clouds, to meet the Lord in the air: and so shall we ever be with the Lord."   1 Thessalonians 2:16-17

Afterwords

—ᴍ—

The foreword (preface) of this book gives a brief statement of why it was written. I examined it and found it to be doctrinally sound, and very interesting.

THE ONE THING I WISH TO ADD is this: The whole Bible is filled with prophecy, with the true history of Israel, with the Psalms, and finally with the story of salvation for the gentiles found in the New Testament. The Jews are NOT excluded from that salvation, however! Why was the Bible written? It is to show us the prophecy of the Coming-Savior, and of the fulfillment of the same! Without the True Messiah, Jesus Christ, there is no true salvation — even many verses, as (see notes below) — Isaiah 53:4-5, show us a preview of the suffering Savior, Jesus, Our Lord! This prophecy is rarely understood by Jesus' own race! We understand He was offered for not just the world's sin, but for me personally. The true theme of the whole Bible is the precious cross and the blood Jesus shed for me and for you. I have studied the Bible full-time for over fifty years, and I see Jesus as the central and great theme of God's Word. Do not read just superficially in the Bible — rather I ask you: OBEY THE GOSPEL! (See I Peter 4: 17) It is as follows:

"WHAT SHALL BE THE END OF THEM THAT OBEY NOT THE GOSPEL", which is the death, burial, and the resurrection of Jesus-Christ. To obey it is first to hear, second to believe, and thirdly to call on the Savior to ask Him to save you, which means you — personally.

"WHOSOEVER SHALL CALL UPON THE NAME OF THE LORD SHALL BE SAVED" is HIS promise to you and for you (See Romans 10:13).

Other Passages concerning the prophesied salvation: Isaiah 53:6, Isaiah 1:18, Genesis 15:6

By a concerned Pastor;

Rev. Dennis R. Herring

Rev. Dennis R. Herring

Printed in the United States
77803LV00004B/8